THE FIRST MODERN CLASH OVER FEDERAL POWER

American Presidential Elections

MICHAEL NELSON

JOHN M. MCCARDELL, JR.

THE FIRST MODERN CLASH OVER FEDERAL POWER

WILSON VERSUS HUGHES IN THE PRESIDENTIAL ELECTION OF 1916

LEWIS L. GOULD

16

UNIVERSITY PRESS OF KANSAS

Published by the University Press of Kansas (Lawrence, Kansas 66045), which was organized by the Kansas Board of Regents and is operated and funded by Emporia State University, Fort Hays State University, Kansas State University, Pittsburg State University, the University of Kansas, and Wichita State University

Library of Congress Cataloging-in-Publication Data

Names: Gould, Lewis L., author.
Title: The first modern clash over federal power : Wilson versus Hughes in the Presidential Election of 1916 / Lewis L. Gould.
Description: Lawrence, Kansas : University Press of Kansas, [2016] | Series: American presidential elections | Includes bibliographical references and index.
Identifiers: LCCN 2016004957
ISBN 9780700622801 (cloth : alk. paper)
ISBN 9780700622818 (ebook)
Subjects: LCSH: Presidents—United States—Election—1916. | Wilson, Woodrow, 1856–1924. | Hughes, Charles Evans, 1862–1948. | Federal government—United States—History—20th century. | United States—Politics and government—1913–1921.
Classification: LCC E769.G68 2016 | DDC 324.973/0913—dc23
LC record available at http://lccn.loc.gov/2016004957.

British Library Cataloguing-in-Publication Data is available.

Printed in the United States of America

10 9 8 7 6 5 4 3 2 1

The paper used in this publication is recycled and contains 30 percent postconsumer waste. It is acid free and meets the minimum requirements of the American National Standard for Permanence of Paper for Printed Library Materials z39.48-1992.

For Jeanne

CONTENTS

EDITORS' FOREWORD

Republicans entered the elections of 1916 confident of victory—and with some reason. The GOP had controlled the House of Representatives for all but four of the last twenty-two years, and had gained sixty-six seats in the 1914 midterm elections. Republican Senate majorities were equally common. The party had won four of the last five presidential elections, all of them convincingly. Republican leaders regarded the one exception to this pattern, Democrat Woodrow Wilson's election in 1912, as a fluke, an artifact of their party's split between conservative supporters of President William Howard Taft and progressive supporters of former president Theodore Roosevelt, both of them Republicans. Between them the Republican nominee, Taft, and TR, running as a third-party candidate, had outpolled Wilson in the national popular vote by 51 percent to 42 percent. In 1916, with Wilson seeking a second term, Republicans were not about to make that mistake again. Instead, they united in support of U.S. Supreme Court Justice Charles Evans Hughes, who had demonstrated his electoral prowess before joining the court by winning elections for governor of New York in 1906 and 1908.

In addition to being a united party in 1916, the GOP regarded the Democrats as a weak one. No Democratic incumbent had been reelected as president since Andrew Jackson in 1828. The Democrats' strongest region was the South, still regarded by many northerners as barely reconstructed after defeat in the Civil War. The Republicans dominated the Northeast, then the most populous and electoral-vote-rich region of the country. New York had forty-five electoral votes, for example, and Pennsylvania had thirty-eight.

Nonetheless, as Lewis Gould explains in this book, the confidence with which Wilson began his bid for a second term was not misplaced. As the head of a united Democratic government for the first time since 1894, he had ridden into office four years earlier with a 435 electoral vote victory and coattails long enough to bring a Democratic majority into Congress. As a strong party leader Wilson was able to pass a raft of progressive legislation, including the Underwood Tariff, the Federal Reserve Act, the Federal Trade Commission Act, and the Clayton Act. The outbreak of the Great War in Europe in 1914 made many Americans reluctant to change leaders in uncertain times, especially with TR campaigning ardently not just for Hughes but also for military preparations that many feared would lead to American involvement in the European war. "Wilson and Peace or Hughes and War" became the Democrats' rallying cry as election day approached in November 1916.

The election was close until the end and even a bit beyond. The outcome in California was narrow, the results late in coming. Whichever candidate won its 13 electoral votes would be president. As Gould shows, Hughes had campaigned ineptly in California, alienating progressive Republican supporters of Governor Hiram Johnson by spending all his time with Johnson's conservative rivals. Wilson carried the state by about 4,000 votes out of nearly a million cast, enough to give him 277 electoral votes to Hughes's 254. The Republicans regained control of the House but the Democrats held on to their majority in the Senate.

As Gould shows, the 1916 elections were noteworthy not just for the Democracy but also for democracy. In 1913, just three years before, the Seventeenth Amendment had transferred the power to select U.S. senators from the state legislatures to the voters. Nineteen sixteen marked the first time popular election of the Senate coincided with a presidential election. In addition, the woman suffrage movement gained strength in 1916, with Hughes supporting what soon became the Nineteenth Amendment and Wilson favoring the reform while preferring that it continue to come about through state action.

Nineteen sixteen also marked the restoration of two-party competition to presidential elections. Gould's book about the 1912 contest is aptly titled *Four Hats in the Ring* because the nominees of the Progressive and Socialist parties joined the Democratic and Republican nominees as viable contenders. In 1916 the Socialist Party nominee, newspaper editor Allen Benson, received just 3 percent of the national popular vote, less than half of Eugene V. Debs's total four years before, and the remnants of the Progressive Party offered no candidate when TR refused to run again as its nominee. Not until 1948 would third-party candidates again be a factor in a presidential election.

Michael Nelson
John McCardell

PREFACE

The presidential election of 1916 has not fared well at the hands of historians. A recent history of the Republican Party covers the contest between Charles Evans Hughes and Woodrow Wilson in a scant three sentences that only touch on the issues between the two parties.[1] The only book on the election is now almost four decades old, and the study that examines one of the electoral implications of the result is nearly thirty years old.[2]

When 1916 is mentioned in popular sources, the judgment usually turns on how close the outcome was and the pivotal role of the state of California in making Wilson victorious. Yet the election had serious ideological consequences for the future of American politics. More even than in the more studied election of 1912, the Republicans and Democrats divided on class-based lines in 1916, with the Wilson campaign in many respects looking forward to the New Deal while the Republicans adopted the small government, anti–labor union, antiregulation positions they have articulated ever since. When Republicans denounced President Wilson for passage of the Adamson Act to forestall a nationwide railroad walkout, they did so for reasons that conservatives now would find very familiar. Convinced that Wilson was illegitimate and a political usurper, the Republicans expected with great confidence that they would win the 1916 election with ease behind their well-qualified candidate, former Supreme Court Justice Charles Evans Hughes. Accustomed to Democratic ineptitude in campaigns, the GOP did not conceive that Wilson could survive. When Hughes proved to be a flawed candidate on the stump and the Democrats put together an efficient campaign, the Republicans found themselves in a close contest where issues of war and peace divided the party and gave the president the upper hand. Wilson prevailed in what has to be regarded as an upset, if not quite on the level of Harry S. Truman in 1948, certainly one that defied contemporary political wisdom.

Victory was a mixed blessing for the Democrats, who saw their fragile electoral coalition collapse under the strains of World War I and Wilson's blunders as a wartime political leader. By 1920 the Republicans regained national power behind Warren G. Harding as the voters repudiated Wilson and his party. Twelve years would elapse before a leader more skilled than Wilson would reassemble the Democrats into what became, with the addition of black Americans, the New Deal coalition. The issues that Franklin D. Roosevelt and his enemies debated, however, would be reminders of 1916 in both language and content. That dialogue would continue until the end of the twentieth century and beyond. In many respects the struggle over government power that Hughes and Wilson waged has never ended. And so the origins of liberal-conservative warfare, so heated in our own time, can be seen on the hustings and in the newspaper columns a century ago in a contest that the confident Republicans expected to win and never really accepted as a defeat.

ACKNOWLEDGMENTS

This book was completed under difficult circumstances and that could not have been accomplished without the kind assistance of valued friends. I suffered a stroke in March 2014 that required months of rehabilitation therapy. While that occurred, research went on for me. I owe special thanks to Kristie Miller for a close reading of the manuscript. Richard McCulley did work on my behalf at the Library of Congress. Other helpful individuals were Maria Fernandez, Hope Grebner, Timothy Mattaz, and Heather Merrill.

At Monmouth College, I owe special thanks to Rick Sayre, Beverly McGuire, and the staff of the Hewes Library for their patience with my many microfilm requests.

Stacy Cordery read the manuscript and offered many useful and timely suggestions for improvement. She has been a thoughtful presence, along with her husband, Simon, and her son, Gareth, for many years, and I owe the Corderys a debt I can never repay.

As I wrote, I gained from the personal kindness of Monmouth and Galesburg friends: Gilbert and Vicki Hennenfent, Peggy and Al Kulczewski, Bob and Carolyn Meling, Owen Muelder, Mary Lou Pease, Mary Phillips, Tom and Anne Sinkewicz, Marilyn Van Hoozer, Kathy Wagoner, Esther White, and Fred and Nancy Witzig. Throughout my career, I have been the beneficiary of the efficiency and professionalism of librarians at the Library of Congress, the Abraham Lincoln Presidential Library, the Perry-Castaneda Library at the University of Texas at Austin, the Massachusetts Historical Society, the Dolph Briscoe Center for American History at the University of Texas at Austin, and numerous other manuscript repositories. I am deeply indebted to them all.

Of course, I alone am responsible for any errors or mistakes in this book and nothing I have written should be ascribed to the kind and caring people who have helped me throughout my career. At Brown I had great teachers—Klaus Epstein, Thomas P. Govan, James B. Hedges, and William G. McLoughlin. Being a historian has been an inspiring and fulfilling experience ever since I entered graduate school at Yale in 1961. I had superb teachers—John Morton Blum, Howard Roberts Lamar, and Elting Morison. So many professional friends—Thomas H. Appleton,

Jr., John Broesamle, Charles Calhoun, Don E. Carleton, John Milton Cooper, Jr., James C. Curtis, Wilton B. Fowler, Gary Gallagher, Gene M. Gressley, Paul Holbo, Laura Kalman, Clarence and Geri Lasby, William Lilley III, the late Herbert F. Margulies, the late Thomas K. McCraw, the late H. Wayne Morgan, Joanne Reitano, William G. Shade, R. Hal Williams, and many others. And students—the late Evan Anders, Bill Childs, Thomas Clarkin, Stacy Cordery, Debbie Cottrell, Patrick Cox, the late Sara Hunter Graham, Byron Hulsey, Jonathan Lee, Anne Hodges Morgan, John Pope, Bradley R. Rice, Craig Roell, and Mark and Nancy Beck Young. It has been a wonderful and rewarding professional life. Finally, I owe thanks to the University Press of Kansas. An author could not have had a more supportive publisher than Fred Woodward and his talented staff through the years. During four decades Karen Gould was a kind, sustaining presence. Now, as they used to say in the profession of my father, -30-.

Lewis L. Gould
Monmouth, Illinois
July 2015

1 THE LEGACY OF 1912

The results of the 1912 election transformed the American political landscape. For the first time in twenty years the Democratic Party, behind the candidacy of Woodrow Wilson, swept into control of the federal government. Wilson secured a landslide victory in the electoral college with 435 votes of forty states to 88 for Theodore Roosevelt and his Progressive Party from six states and a mere 8 electoral votes for the incumbent chief executive, William Howard Taft, from the small states of Utah and Vermont.

For all its prominence in the literature of American politics, however, the 1912 contest did not feature serious differences between the Republicans and the Democrats. Woodrow Wilson and his party focused for the most part on the challenge that Theodore Roosevelt and the Progressives presented in the shape of Roosevelt's New Nationalism. Wilson countered with his New Freedom, which advocated reform without a great expansion of governmental power. The demoralized Republicans, with President Taft hardly campaigning, relied on their customary advocacy of the tariff as the main part of their appeal. There was a dearth of ideological intensity between the two major parties in 1912.

When the results came in, the Republicans concluded that the Taft-Roosevelt split, not differences with the Democrats, had been their downfall. The Democratic candidate had secured only 41.9 percent of the popular vote. Meanwhile, Roosevelt had garnered 27.4

percent while Taft had tallied 23.2 percent. Adding the votes of Roosevelt and Taft together convinced many Republicans that their party's underlying majority, established during the 1890s, could once again be restored with a popular candidate who could unify the GOP. There was no need to depart from their customary pro-tariff appeal to defeat the Democrats.

For the Republicans the electoral problem ran deeper. The Democrats, who had been gaining since their overwhelming defeat in 1904, held control of both houses of Congress. In the House, Wilson and his party had added sixty-one new members to their majority first achieved in 1910. They controlled the Senate by 51–44. The Democrats, if they stayed united, could enact Wilson's New Freedom program of tariff revision and banking reform. When the Democrats did so, the Republicans found themselves in new and unfamiliar political circumstances.

Until that began to happen, the defeated parties could only engage in elaborate post-mortems. For Roosevelt's Progressives, the question was whether they could supplant the Republicans as the major party alternative to the Democrats. On the surface the new party could make a good case that their start was better and more promising than any other comparable organization in the country's history such as the Republicans in the mid-1850s. From nowhere in June 1912 they had established a presence nationally and elected seventeen of their number to the House of Representatives. With Theodore Roosevelt as their leader they had instant credibility and access to the national press. As Roosevelt himself said, "I firmly believe that we have put forward the cause of justice and humanity by many years."[1]

On the other hand, the Moosers, as they were known after Roosevelt's assertion in 1912 that he felt like a Bull Moose, recognized that their appeal rested on Roosevelt's personal charisma. Their reform ideas had gotten a hearing because of their presidential candidate's appeal as an individual. What would happen if Roosevelt's personal life took him in new directions, wondered many who had followed him on his quest for the White House and who believed in his reform program.

The Republicans contemplated an even more uncertain future. In the three-party contest they had finished a dismal third with their candidates repudiated. The Wilson tide and Republican divisions had swept away such party stalwarts as former Speaker of the House Joseph G. Cannon and Theodore Roosevelt's son-in-law, Nicholas Longworth. Cannon told a friend that "the party landed in Purgatory from which place according to orthodox teaching there is an escape. We have to be thankful we didn't land in that other place from which it is said there is no escape."[2]

The electoral disaster and Roosevelt's departure intensified the debate within the Grand Old Party about its future as an organization. There had been serious qualms about Roosevelt's belief in more government regulation even before he bolted. His advocacy of the recall of judicial decisions through popular votes in 1912 had been a breaking point for many conservatives. Now, regular party members maintained that "if the Republican party is to have a future it must be on conservative lines: it must be the great conservative party of the nation."[3]

Other voices among Republicans expressed similar views. William A. Barnes, the leader of the New York party, wrote in his newspaper that "the Republican Party must and will stand up on its own ground. There will be no compromise with those who are antagonistic to its principles." Joseph G. Cannon told the press: "The Republican Party is not dead. I hope that all those who believe in the policy of the party will unite with it."[4]

Political calculations bolstered the convictions of Republican regulars in early 1913. GOP stalwarts had long believed that the Democrats would blunder at some crucial point to give the Republicans an opening. It had been an article of faith among Republican partisans that the Democrats, inept and illegitimate, chronically made crucial mistakes that cost them political points. "My experience with the Democratic party," wrote William Howard Taft in mid-April 1913, "has been in matters requiring capacity for government that whatever they did was wrong."[5] In 1893, after winning the presidency and control of both houses of Congress, the Democrats under Grover Cleveland had mishandled the economic depression arising from the Panic of 1893, the Wilson-Gorman Tariff, and the silver question. The result had been sweeping Republican victories in the elections of 1894 and 1896. The party regulars expected that the novice Wilson, elected as an accident, would experience a similar result in 1914 and be voted out of office in 1916. The GOP had only to wait for Democratic mistakes to regain its political dominance. The party newly in power posed no long-term ideological threat to the GOP.

So when proposals surfaced for the Republicans and Progressives to reunite, the Republicans saw no reason for hasty action. The most public of these schemes came from the wealthy newspaper publisher Frank A. Munsey, who had been one of the major financial backers of Roosevelt in 1912. He used his newspapers and periodicals to advance "amalgamation" between the anti-Wilson forces. Munsey envisioned a "holding party" that would grow out of state conventions of Progressives and Republicans, which would in turn select delegates to a meeting of the new party that would then oppose the Democrats. He saw in the future "the 'Liberal' party" as a result of this process. He stressed that he had not discussed his ideas with Theodore Roosevelt.[6]

Any hopes that Munsey might have had about Roosevelt's receptivity to "amalgamation" soon disappeared. Shattered by his election defeat, Roosevelt had revived the grievances against Taft and the conservatives that had impelled him to run as a third-party candidate in 1912. Within a day, a statement came from Roosevelt renewing his criticism of the Republicans and reaffirming his commitment to the Progressive Party. "Personally, I strongly feel that we should no more enter into a combination with the Republican machine than with the Democratic machine." A speech by President Taft defending his renomination in 1912 drew Roosevelt's ire. He denounced the president's convention victory as "barefaced political theft and fraud" and once again claimed that his own nomination "was deliberately stolen from the people by the bosses on behalf of the privileged interests." He charged again as he had not done for some months that in key states such as Arizona and Washington the regulars had practiced fraud and theft. Roosevelt reaffirmed his allegiance to the Progressives, which he maintained throughout 1913. As he wrote an old political friend, "I believe firmly that ninety per cent of the Republican party would like to follow our lead or have a coalition with us on the basis of our platform. But I do not see how it is to be achieved under the present Republican leadership."[7]

With Roosevelt committed to the Progressives for the moment, any impulse for changing party procedures among Republicans failed. As the *New-York Tribune* put it, the theory of the regular leaders was "that the party will be restored through the blunders of the Democracy in power and through the natural gravitation of the Progressives back to their old allegiance."[8] When Senator Elihu Root of New York and former Massachusetts senator Winthrop Murray Crane called for a national convention in the fall of 1913, it attracted some interest, but most Republicans saw no reason to act. As anticipated, the Progressives had already experienced a falling-off in their vote in local elections and Democrats faced potential divisions as they sought to implement tariff reform and banking legislation.

One major issue was the nature of the Grand Old Party in southern states. Because of the allegiance of the Democrats to segregation in all aspects of life, the Republicans were shut out of any hope of winning electoral votes in the region. In presidential elections, the Democrats started out with more than 130 electoral votes before any ballots were counted. Critics of the existing system asked why southern Republicans should not have a lesser voice in nominating presidential candidates. In response to these criticisms, the party decided to reduce the number of delegates from the South to the national convention in a modest but not sweeping manner.[9]

The Republicans were in a bind in 1913–1914 in appealing to southerners. The Wilson presidency and the Democrats in general were still champions of white supremacy in Dixie. There was no way for the Republicans to compete for the allegiance of white southerners before the New Deal. The African American vote in the North stayed with the Grand Old Party as the Great Migration brought more and more black southerners northward. Moreover, the segregationist policies of the Wilson administration kept blacks loyal to the Republicans. In time these new residents of northern cities would abandon the Republicans but that had not yet happened in the early years of Wilson's administration.

For the Republicans, the achievements of Wilson in office produced some surprising and unwelcome results. The Grand Old Party was not prepared for a strong Democratic chief executive who did things. The last time that had happened had been during Grover Cleveland's first term from 1885 to 1889, outside the political memory of most Republicans. Wilson delivered a compelling inaugural address and then summoned Congress into special session to deal with the tariff. He announced that he would deliver his tariff message in person, breaking with a century-old precedent that had precluded chief executives from appearing in the flesh before lawmakers.[10] Using publicity and personal suasion, Wilson proceeded to confound skeptics in Washington and pushed the Underwood Tariff through Congress, lowering rates and instituting an income tax without splitting the Democrats. The administration had, said a popular magazine, "done much to remove the grounds for the criticism which has been consistently and justly against their party in the past that it is incapable of positive action."[11] One Republican senator concluded: "There is no doubt that Mr. Wilson is showing himself a very adroit politician."[12]

Throughout the legislative maneuvering that resulted in the Underwood Tariff, the opposition to the president and the Democrats expressed increasing dismay about Wilson's tactics. A Republican journalist and one of William Howard Taft's close friends, Gus Karger, told the former president that "the gentleman from Princeton seems to have Congress thoroughly 'buffaloed' and 'government by intimidation' would be an apposite title for the chapter in American history that is now being written."[13] Forgetting that they had given the Democrats no role in tariff making when they had a majority, Republicans now denounced the Democratic reliance on the party caucus. Senator Joseph L. Bristow of Kansas contended that "if the caucus system which has been adopted by the Democrats had been used by the Republicans in forcing through the Payne-Aldrich bill it would have created a howl throughout the country that would have been deafening."[14]

Bristow had a short memory. Republicans in the House and Senate had limited the role of the Democrats in the framing of the Payne-Aldrich Tariff in 1909. When they were in power the Republicans had routinely excluded the minority from meaningful participation in the affairs of the House. The objection in 1913–1914 was that the Democrats were being effective as the majority for the first time in years.

Although he had spoken of seeking "common counsel" in his inaugural address, Wilson proved to be a president who rarely relied on the advice of the politicians who came to see him. He listened politely to visitors but rarely acted on what they told him if it differed from his personal convictions. Politicians soon noticed this Wilsonian trait and shared with colleagues their views of the president's tendencies. Senator William P. Dillingham of Vermont informed a reporter friend: "The President, as you know, is the most self-contained man whom any of us have ever seen in office. Apparently he shares his confidence with no one outside of the Democratic party, and sparingly with the individual members of that party."[15] Taft complained, as did other Republicans, that "the trouble about Wilson is that he knows it all and nobody can tell him anything."[16] Reasonable criticism would soon turn bitter.

Convinced that as the natural governing party of the nation they deserved to be consulted and their advice heeded, Republicans bridled when Wilson functioned as a partisan chief executive. An early episode fanned Republican suspicions of the new president. Congress dealt with appropriations in the Sundry Civil Bill in April 1913.The American Federation of Labor, led by Samuel Gompers, had been a strong supporter of the Democrats since 1906. Now they sought their reward. They wanted language in the Sundry bill that would bar the Justice Department from using the injunctive power in the Sherman Antitrust Act against the AFL in labor disputes. Conservatives saw the wielding of injunctions in strikes as a needed weapon against labor anarchy.[17]

Frustrated in passing such a bill on its own, the new Democratic majority crafted wording for the Sundry Bill that achieved labor's aim. Wilson decided to sign the bill despite the pro-union wording. He did so in language that his major biographer called unconvincing. Conservatives reacted with outrage at what seemed to them a chief executive giving in to lawlessness.[18] William Howard Taft believed the incident showed that Wilson "is not governed nearly so much by principle as he would have people believe" and he denounced "that outrageous discrimination in favor of trades-unions and farmers in the matter of the enforcement of the anti-trust law."[19] If the Democrats started to woo specific interest groups, they would be challenging the Republican belief that the government should not cater to individual sectors of society. Other aspects of Wilson's partisan approach did not sit well with the opposition and stirred rancor for the GOP. Republicans took pride in the quality of the diplomatic service they had established during the Roosevelt and Taft administrations. They watched with more than a little dismay as Wilson turned diplomatic appointments over to Secretary of State William Jennings Bryan, who in turn found places for men whom Bryan called "deserving Democrats," many with scant qualifications for their new jobs. Wilson did not go all the way with Bryan's patronage approach but the quality of the diplomatic service did decline during the Wilson years. Though the Republicans made much of the issue, especially during the 1916 election, the criticism did not resonate with the public.

The Republicans took particular pride in their relationship with the Philippines. Under William Howard Taft (1900–1904) and other GOP proconsuls, Republican leaders believed they had given the islands wise, nonpartisan leadership toward eventual independence at some distant, unspecified date. Democrats on the other hand were convinced that the acquisition of the archipelago in 1898 had been a serious mistake and that the United States should relinquish control of the Philippines once the residents had displayed the capacity for self-government. Wilson eventually named a member of Congress from New York, Francis Burton Harrison, as governor general of the Philippines to implement the Democratic program of giving the Filipinos a greater part in their own affairs. President Taft had barred Harrison from the White House over his partisan criticism and the former president regarded Harrison as a shady character in his personal life. The appointment and subsequent Democratic legislation looking toward Philippine independence sharpened the animosities between the two parties.[20]

In the battles that ensued over the tariff in 1913, the Republicans defended their protectionist record and contended that Democratic tariff reduction would lead to a slowing economy and an eventual depression. The imposition of an income tax to compensate for reduced revenues arising from lower customs duties started the Republicans on their commitment to diminished taxes and smaller government that would become a hallmark of their party. By 1914, Republicans were complaining that Wilson was an antibusiness president who had "put through a dangerous and destructive legislative program."[21]

Another area that the Republicans sought to exploit against the Democrats in 1913–1914 was Mexico. There the long-standing government of Porfirio Díaz had succumbed to a popular revolution led by the reformer Francisco Madero. In the waning days of the Taft administration, opponents of Madero had ousted him and then killed him. Wilson refused to recognize the leader of the coup, Victoriano Huerta, as the legitimate government in Mexico City. Republicans questioned Wilson's strategy and the resulting failure to protect the lives and property of Americans in Mexico while running the risk of war.

An indefinable element in the political controversies of the early Wilson administration was the personal animus that Republican leaders developed toward the president as an individual. Joseph L. Bristow called Wilson "a sheep in wolf's clothing" who was "more ultra reactionary than Taft or Ben Harrison ever were." Elihu Root, William Howard Taft, and Henry Cabot Lodge all concluded early on in their dealings with Wilson that he could not be trusted. The president was artful in his manipulation of words in his public statements and often practiced what he called "grazing the truth" in his dealings with reporters and fellow politicians. By 1915 Lodge was telling Theodore Roosevelt that he "never expected to hate anyone in politics with the hatred I feel towards Wilson."[22] An illegitimate usurper in the eyes of many Republicans, Wilson was not entitled to the respect that surrounded his office. Instead, he should be opposed with every possible weapon and driven from office in 1916.

Theodore Roosevelt, too, had come to despise Wilson as a result of their exchanges in the 1912 campaign. "I don't like Wilson or trust him," Roosevelt told an English friend in 1913, "and I think Bryan a flamboyant ass."[23] In the aftermath of his defeat in the 1912 election, Roosevelt re-

Henry Cabot Lodge. The Massachusetts senator and lifelong friend of Theodore Roosevelt became the most bitter Republican enemy of President Woodrow Wilson. Courtesy of the Library of Congress.

mained committed to the Progressive Party he had created as the vehicle for his presidential ambitions. He wanted to run again in 1916 to beat Wilson and return to the power that made him fully alive. To do that, however, he had to keep the Progressive Party functioning since any resumption of relations with the Republicans seemed impossible after his apostasy. Yet Roosevelt's skills as a party builder were at best marginal as his second term in the White House had shown.

In the weeks following the election of 1912, members of the Progressive Party recognized their predicament and their dependence on Roosevelt. Harold Ickes of Chicago posed the salient question to Amos Pinchot, a fellow Progressive, in a letter in early December. "Lacking the enthusiasm of a national campaign and the leadership on the stump of Col. Roosevelt, can we continue to arouse interest in support of our Progressive program?"[24]

The problem was that the Progressives, as Ickes recognized, were at the mercy of Wilson's success or failure as a future president. The assumption was that the Democrats had reactionary elements that would outweigh any reform impulse from the new chief executive. But what if Wilson exceeded expectations? "I have no hesitancy in saying that if we have a thoroughly Progressive administration under President Wilson our party is likely to have a brief life."[25]

As a result of Wilson's unexpected success in enacting the Democratic agenda, Theodore Roosevelt faced a complex set of circumstances in the waning months of 1913. Since leaving the White House, the former president had not displayed the sure political touch that he had possessed in office. He had cut his ties with the Republicans, his traditional political home. If he wished to seek the White House again in 1916, the Progressives were his only real option. Psychologically troubled at his loss in the election, Roosevelt had little time to rebound from the defeat before the leaders of his third party fell to squabbling among themselves about the conduct of the election and the future course of the party.

The most immediate issue was the role of the New York financier and close Roosevelt friend, George W. Perkins. Associated in the public mind with the large corporations he had formed as a partner with J. P. Morgan, Perkins seemed an improbable advocate for Progressive ideals to such Progressive stalwarts as Amos and Gifford Pinchot. They assailed his prominent place in the party in post-election letters to Roosevelt. Whatever the merits of the complaints from the Pinchot brothers, their timing could not have been worse in terms of the public image of the Progressive Party. As Roosevelt later complained, "Reformers are a dreadful set, and it is awfully hard to try to do anything with them!"[26] The inescapable fact was, as Frank Munsey told former Indiana senator Albert J. Beveridge, "there is no considerable money in the Progressive Party, save in the pockets of a very few, and the very few will not feel called upon to fight another campaign alone."[27]

During the 1912 campaign, the articulate and dynamic Perkins had been second only to Roosevelt as a public advocate of the new party. He made good copy at the New York headquarters and reporters found him an easy source to quote. The visibility that Perkins achieved did not suit other leading Progressives. "He was a tremendous load for us to carry during the campaign," Harold Ickes wrote later.[28] To critics of Perkins, there was something incongruous in having a major figure in the business world, on the boards of International Harvester and U.S. Steel, occupy such a visible role in the reform effort.

With the votes counted and the party defeated, these long-simmering animosities came to the distraught Roosevelt for resolution. The volatile Pinchot brothers suggested to Roosevelt that the headquarters of the Progressives be moved to Washington and a senator of Progressive sympathies be placed in charge of the party's organization. They wanted Perkins "kept in the background."[29]

There was little doubt about how Roosevelt would decide the Perkins flap. The financier was one of Roosevelt's closest political friends and a major contributor to the coffers of the Progressives. The dispute ended in a conference of Progressives in Chicago in December 1912 where Roosevelt sustained his friend within the party. Perkins emerged from the meeting stronger than ever in party councils.

The effort to make the Progressive Party a viable organization went forward during the first half of 1913 under arduous and often adverse political circumstances. Believing that voters who had defected in 1912 would drift back to their customary roots, the Republicans did little to make life easier for Roosevelt and his allies. Meanwhile, the Democrats carried forward their program and saw no reason to conciliate what appeared to them an ineffectual rump of the Republicans. The Progressives struggled to gain traction as a credible alternative to the two major parties.

The plight of the seventeen Progressive members of the House underscored the problem. Impotent against the huge Democratic majority, the Progressives stood against the rate-reducing Underwood Tariff and thus just seemed a variant of traditional Republican protectionism rather than a group with new fresh ideas. When Roosevelt conceded that the Democratic tariff proposal was "a little better" than the Payne-Aldrich Tariff of 1909 but there was no real difference between the two measures, his comments rang hollow since there was no chance of achieving the tariff commission answer that the third party favored. How did the Progressives differ from the GOP if they took a protectionist position?[30]

Below the national level, the Progressives did some good work on behalf of woman suffrage and political reform in the states. The labors of such reformers as Frances Kellor and Donald Richberg were creditable but non-exciting. The key to the success of the party lay with their one sure-fire drawing card—Roosevelt himself. By 1913 Roosevelt had become a political celebrity. Offers and requests poured into his office in an endless flood that simply swamped his ability to respond in a timely manner. He worried about the consequences for himself and his career from over-exposure. Roosevelt told a Progressive colleague "that he should not be used except for a very few occasions, each use diminished just so much of his power of attraction and influence."[31] As voter interest waned and the total of the party fell off in local elections, it became apparent that Roosevelt was all that the Progressive party really offered to the country.

And Roosevelt had competing personal priorities that took time away from his commitment to the fortunes of the Progressives. Long angered by the whispering campaign that called him a drunkard, Roosevelt had determined in 1912 to refute these rumors in a public forum. He and his lawyers filed a libel suit against an obscure Michigan editor who printed the charges that Roosevelt drank. The case came to trial in late May 1913. Numerous witnesses attested that Roosevelt consumed tiny amounts of liquor at infrequent intervals. The jury ruled in favor of Roosevelt who sought only nominal damages and the restoration of his reputation.

By the summer of 1913 Roosevelt was deep into planning for a trip to South America in the latter part of the year and the early months of 1914. In a kind of replay of his 1909–1910 African adventure, Roosevelt sought to recapture the vigor and élan of his youth one final time. That the trip represented what he called his last chance to be a boy again attested to the juvenile element in Roosevelt's thinking. In reality, he was a corpulent man in his fifties who tended to overeat, and was blind in one eye, and in poor physical shape. A physically taxing exploration of the interior of the Amazon would have been dubious for a young man in peak physical condition. For Roosevelt it was beyond quixotic.

Beyond those hard facts was the issue of what he owed to the Progressive Party. In 1912 he had asked politicians all over the country to follow him out of the Republican ranks and into his third-party venture. They had done so in the confidence that Roosevelt, with his abundant personal appeal to the voters, would lead them in the 1912 presidential race and beyond. Now the Progressive leader would be out of the country and away from the political fray at a time when their party most needed his leadership.

The Brazilian trip was a personal disaster for Roosevelt. His explorations brought him physical perils that led him to the brink of death. His son Kermit, along to safeguard his father's well-being, refused at crucial moments in the danger-filled journey to see the elder Roosevelt left behind. The former president survived but undermined his health to the extent that he never regained a good physical condition for the few years he had left. He came back to New York in May 1914 after his ordeal and everyone recognized that the ailing, limping figure, supported by a cane, had been through extraordinary circumstances that had shattered his resilience. One reporter concluded: "He looks like hell."[32] Yet almost at once he was expected to throw himself into the congressional races of 1914 to stave off defeat for the weakened Progressive Party. There were calls for him to run for governor of New York and to speak all over the country.

During Roosevelt's months away from the United States, the political tide seemed to be running well in favor of the Republicans. The Democrats and Wilson had continued the pursuit of their ambitious agenda. Having revised the tariff downward, the lawmakers, with the president prodding them for action, had enacted banking reform through the Federal Reserve Act in late 1913. While the consensus was that the *banking* law was needed, the process of enacting it spent some of Wilson's political capital. The Republicans anticipated a normal voter reaction against a newly elected president and the Democratic congressional majority as 1913 went on.

The off-year elections in 1913 had revealed no clear trend against the Wilson administration. Indeed the White House was pleased that Democrats won the governorships in Massachusetts and Maryland. Former president Taft noted the falling off of the Progressive vote in Bridgeport, Connecticut. He was equally gratified with the poor showing of Augustus P. Gardner, son-in-law of Henry Cabot Lodge, in the Massachusetts gubernatorial contest. It was, Taft wrote, "a very considerable jolt" for "that element in the Republican party that thinks that the views of the conservative part of the party can be disregarded by a union in which we are to surrender to the Progressive element in the party who are just as radical as the Progressives themselves."[33]

The economy was sluggish and some GOP members took the predictable course of blaming tariff reduction for any hard times. In the House, the Republicans through their leader, James R. Mann of Illinois, sought to harry the Democrats in December 1913 when Mann alleged that "the country is in the midst of a financial and industrial panic."[34] Mann had a point. Business failures in October 1913 were running at levels not seen since the depression of the 1890s. Other Republicans echoed Mann's theme as his party followed its time-tested script in attacking the party in power. By the spring of 1914 the Republicans sensed that the tide of public opinion was moving in their direction while the Democrats worried over their prospects before the voters.

The New Freedom of Wilson had been a three-pronged promise of legislative action—the tariff, banking and currency, and antitrust reform. The first two had been achieved in a prolonged congressional session in 1913 and, as 1914 began, the president insisted that Congress act on the problem of industrial consolidation and consider the antitrust legislation the Democrats in Congress were preparing. The administration was actually moving in opposite directions, trying to fulfill its campaign promises to curb business at a time when the president was becoming more and more convinced "that the only danger that threatens his administration is from depressed business conditions."[35]

That prospect was enough to terrify Democrats who recalled how their party had suffered during the 1890s when Grover Cleveland had mishandled the Panic of 1893 and the party experienced devastating losses in the 1894 congressional contests. They could see the scenario appearing all over again with the same dire result. To counteract the Republican onslaught, Democrats in the House, led by Speaker Champ Clark, rebutted the assaults of Mann and other Republicans with promises of good times to come as a result of lowering the tariff and the newly enacted Federal Reserve Law. "There is a big business boom coming as sure as shooting," Clark observed in late December 1913.[36]

Wilson himself followed a conciliatory policy toward business during the first half of 1913. There were statements from the White House about his willingness to meet in person with business operators. A reporter in February 1914 struck just the note that the administration wanted: "Business has nothing to fear from Mr. Wilson so long as he continues his present course."[37]

The president, who was not a radical man by nature, no doubt was sincere in his professions of sympathy for entrepreneurs and their concerns during the early months of 1914. Yet there was something forced and artificial about Wilson's reassuring comments. He had no background in business himself, having been a college professor and university president all his adult life. He had friends in the business world such as the wealthy Cleveland H. Dodge, who had donated so generously to Wilson's campaigns. His closest advisor, Edward M. House of Texas, had an affinity for capitalists. Yet the Republicans, with their close ties to the world of enterprise and finance, could always demonstrate a greater sense of fellow feeling with the rank and file of the business world. The growing animosity toward Wilson and his party permeated the business world.

Champ Clark and the president promised in late 1913 and early 1914 that the Democratic Congress would proceed with its extensive legislative agenda including reform of the Sherman Antitrust Act. The events of the first half of 1914 emboldened the Republicans and did not help the Democrats with the voters. In 1912 Congress had passed legislation that exempted American ships from paying tolls on the Panama Canal, which was scheduled to begin its operation in 1914. The law clearly violated the Hay-Pauncefote Treaty of 1901 that put all shipping through the canal on an equal footing. The law produced diplomatic difficulties with the British, and Wilson asked Congress for repeal.

Many Democrats, including the House leadership, favored the law's retention, as the 1912 Democratic platform had promised, and the issue split the Democratic caucus. Republicans rejoiced at the prospect of serious divisions within the majority coalition. The tolls issue was a volatile one on which passions ran high. Wilson's about-face from the 1912 Democratic platform aroused strong opposition in the country and seemed for a time to threaten a Democratic split in Congress. Wilson prevailed at the cost of some lingering hard feelings in his own party and a boost for the GOP. In New Jersey, in a special congressional election, the Republican candidate achieved a decisive victory on April 7, 1914, in what was seen as a test of sentiment against repeal of the Canal toll law.[38] Republicans boasted in the House that they would prevail in the fall elections and retake the lower chamber.[39]

A subsidiary event in the tolls controversy revealed the bad feelings that now flowed between ordinary Republicans and the president. In a House speech on March 29, Representative Joseph R. Knowland, a California Republican, looked at meetings of Wilson and British diplomats over the preceding months and inquired whether the president had made a trade with Great Britain over the tolls issue in return for help with Mexico. The allegation was described in the White House by the president himself as the "crowning insult" of the tolls fight and a direct assault on Wilson's personal integrity. One gleeful Republican wrote in private the day after Knowland floated his thoughts: "Wilson is charged with having been euchred by the British and with now demanding an unconditional surrender to our ancient foe and rival and there is no telling where it will end. The day of his domination of Congress is over, unless I am mistaken."[40]

Knowland, who assumed Wilson's guilt, was premature and wrong. Wilson won his victory and the issue of an alleged deal with England

Elihu Root. The former secretary of state under Theodore Roosevelt, Root had little respect for Woodrow Wilson and hoped to see him ousted in 1916. Courtesy of the Library of Congress.

faded away. That the president had all but called the House Republicans liars did not go away. The conviction grew within the Grand Old Party that Wilson's duplicity and dishonesty was an essential part of his character. A Republican journalist wrote to a colleague in early May 1914: "It is impossible for me to express the disgust I feel at the ineptitude of this administration. I met Senator Root this morning and he feels the same as we do."[41] And Root had been one of Wilson's strongest Republican allies during the tolls fight.

On two other subjects, Republican suspicion of Wilson was always very close to the surface. In the disputes over Mexican policy, Republicans stood with the president in April 1914 when he sought congressional support to intervene in that country over the arrest of American sailors at the port of Vera Cruz, which in turn persuaded Wilson to confront the regime of Victoriano Huerta with armed force. Though Congress went along with the president and the Republicans joined in "with disgust in our mouths" to back Wilson, Republicans took a more militant posture than the Democrats toward events in Mexico and would extend that policy into the presidential contest of 1916.

Coupled with their ongoing indictment of the White House for its alleged attacks on business confidence, the Republicans now garnered most of the headlines as the main opposition to the Wilson administration. One Progressive Party leader noted in a wry moment in January 1914, "So far the Republicans have managed to occupy the front of the stage in antagonism to the Democracy."[42]

As spring 1914 proceeded, the Republicans felt a growing sense of confidence about their prospects in the fall elections. In late June a prominent banker wrote that "the administration is losing support at an astonishing rate."[43] Some erosion of popular backing for the president was to be expected two years after winning the White House. Wilson also suffered from a worldwide economic downturn that the opposition blamed on the Underwood Tariff for undermining confidence in the future of American business and threatening national prosperity. The battle over the Panama Canal tolls irritated the public and its harmful effects on the Democrats lingered on into the fall. American politics seemed to be returning to its customary pattern and the Republican electoral majority was reasserting itself after the anomaly of 1912.

On June 28, 1914, the *Washington Post* published a lengthy analysis of the Democratic electoral woes and noted that Republicans were looking for a repeat of the election of 1894 when their party swept the board against the Cleveland administration.[44] The predictions of a Republican sweep, while well grounded, rested on the assumption that American politics would remain in familiar grooves. However, had a reader of the newspaper earlier that Sunday morning in late June purchased an evening edition of a newspaper in the nation's capital, they would also have seen a banner headline that read: "Serb Student Assassinates Archduke and His Duchess."[45] World War I was about to begin and the course of American politics and the election of 1916 were destined to follow new and untested paths. World War I would complicate and then frustrate entirely Republican efforts to defeat Woodrow Wilson and get him out of office.

2

THE 1914 ELECTION, THE GREAT WAR, AND BEYOND

American politicians were no more ready than their European counterparts to understand what caused the outbreak of World War I in August 1914. The crisis that emerged after the murders of Archduke Francis Ferdinand and his wife in Sarajevo on June 28, 1914, led over the next month to an all-out European conflict that defied all expectations of a permanent lasting peace among the great powers. How such a war would affect the United States was a question no one could answer. As the opening moves of the fighting unfolded it became clear that the previous assumptions about the course of partisan politics would also be soon changed.

The nation turned to President Woodrow Wilson for indications of how best to respond to the shocking news. Wilson told the nation, separated from the war by the Atlantic Ocean, the United States must "be neutral in fact as well as in name during these times that are to try men's souls. We must be impartial in thought as well as in action, must put a curb on our sentiments."[1] While partisans of the warring powers criticized Wilson, he probably reflected American opinion.

The president was under great personal strain in these weeks. His wife, Ellen Wilson, who had been ill for several months, had just died from the effects of Bright's disease, and Wilson was an emotional wreck at her passing. He sought solace in the demands of his work against the pain of his intense grief.

In a political sense the onset of the war offered the

Democrats an opportunity to do what losing politicians so often want and seldom receive—-a chance to change the subject. In the turmoil that accompanied the fighting, they seized the opportunity to ask voters to rally around the president and his leadership. Earlier efforts to do that on the basis of domestic issues had not worked, but now the Democrats could play a card denied to them in the past—patriotism. As Gus Karger noted somewhat ruefully to former president Taft in early September: "The war, I fear, has obliterated many of the issues that seemed clear-cut six weeks ago."[2] The tariff and business conditions, key elements in the Republican appeal, receded in the popular mind. Once again, for the GOP, Wilson's political luck enabled him to slip away from what Republicans regarded as his deserved political fate.

Wilson himself, not much inclined to overt partisanship in the conduct of his office, announced in early September that he would not be taking the stump on behalf of Democratic congressional candidates. He would instead "stay on the job" and perform the duties of the presidency in midst of the new world crisis. Meanwhile the Democrats, backed by letters from the White House, would tell the voters about "the Democratic record of achievement, the clearing away of all doubt and uncertainty that have plagued business, the wiping out of any further antagonism between the government and the industrial agencies of the country, and the clearing of the track for unprecedented prosperity."[3]

In further public letters to Democratic candidates, Wilson elaborated on the record of his party. "The Democratic party is now in fact the only instrument ready to the country's hand by which anything can be accomplished." The Republicans, for their part, were "utterly unserviceable as an instrument of reform." The Democrats used the letter of the president to Representative Oscar W. Underwood as their major document in the fall campaign and sought to make Wilson himself the focus of the party's appeal.[4]

This act of presidential self-denial about campaigning and his reliance on letters from the White House represented only part of the Democratic appeal to the electorate. In the campaign textbook that the Democratic National Committee issued for the use of its candidates, the leading slogan, featured on the first page of the publication, was "War in the East! Peace in the West! Thank God for Wilson!"[5] While the president stayed in the White House and wrote public letters to Democratic hopefuls, cabinet officers fanned out across the country in what the *Washington Post* called "active participation in the congressional campaign."[6]

The keynote was the request to stand by the president and support his policies on domestic issues and the war itself. Even the Springfield *Republican* said "it would be a misfortune to deprive him of the support and freedom which a friendly Congress would give to him." The war, many papers concluded, had changed the political dynamic and taken away the sting from issues such as the tariff.[7]

The cabinet officers who served as presidential surrogates did not hold back in their praise of the White House incumbent. Secretary of State William Jennings Bryan told American mothers that the president "would rather your sons would live for their country than die on foreign soil in an unnecessary war." Speaker Champ Clark argued that historians would say that Wilson's efforts to keep his country out of war "constituted his clearest title to the gratitude of his country."[8]

The Democrats were now in unfamiliar territory. During the Civil War and the war with Spain in 1898 they had been on the receiving end of numerous Republican appeals to endorse a war president and his policies as an act of patriotism. Then, disagreement or dissent gave the Republicans a chance to make direct attacks against the legitimacy of their opposition. Now the Democrats were in power and the issue of supporting the president worked in their favor. This sudden switch of roles left the Republicans somewhat wrong-footed. Their indictment of the Underwood Tariff sounded dry and a little irrelevant in the face of marching armies and the threats to the American economy. Yet the opposition party lacked a clear, consistent position on what should be done about issues of neutrality and supporting the president. It was a dilemma that persisted for the next two years. Nonetheless, Republicans of all stripes expected a sweeping victory and perhaps GOP control of both houses of Congress once the results came in.

As the war went on, a split emerged among Republicans that would become more intense as the fighting continued. Some party leaders in the East concluded that a victorious Germany would pose a direct threat to the future security of the country. They based that judgment on the way Germany had behaved in the war from the outset. Elihu Root believed, for example, that "if ever a war occurred in which the cause of civilization is represented by one side to the controversy, the present war furnishes an example."[9] To this faction, the menace of Germany was so clear that immediate American intervention on the Allied side was justified.

Theodore Roosevelt, not yet returned to the Republican ranks, came, after an initial period of neutrality, to such an anti-German position that his strident views seemed likely to produce a confrontation with Berlin. He was especially critical of the cautious policies of Wilson and Secretary of State Bryan, whom he regarded with hatred and contempt. Wilson was a worse foreign-policy president in Roosevelt's mind than either Thomas Jefferson or James Buchanan, two historical figures who had earned Roosevelt's particular scorn.

Roosevelt had a soul mate in his old friend Senator Henry Cabot Lodge of Massachusetts. Committed to the same kind of vigorous foreign policy that Roosevelt espoused, Lodge did not take long to reach an anti-German position on the war. He also came to have an equally low opinion of Wilson as a diplomatist. Lodge and his son-in-law, Representative Augustus P. "Gussie" Gardner of Massachusetts, favored a strong stance in preparing the nation to defend itself against potential German aggression.[10]

But the belligerent voices on the East Coast were not the whole of the Republican Party as the world war broke out. Across the Middle West in states such as Iowa, Wisconsin, and Missouri, millions of German-American voters formed a reliable bloc of Republican votes. If the 1916 presidential election should be close, these states and others would provide electoral votes the GOP would need against the president. Progressive Republicans, stronger in the Middle West, wanted neutrality and peace and saw little to be gained from Roosevelt's bellicose posture. These alignments would solidify as the neutrality period went on.

Though there were no modern opinion polls to measure public sentiment in the autumn of 1914, historians agree that throughout the nation Wilson's posture of neutrality enjoyed broad support. Americans rooted for the success of specific European nations, whether the Allies or the Central Powers, but they did not wish to be drawn into the conflict as a combatant nation.

In the elections, several high-profile contests dominated news coverage and the response of the voters encouraged Republicans about their long-run hopes to beat Wilson. This was the first election in which voters would select senators by popular vote since the Seventeenth Amendment had gone into effect the preceding year. A battle noted with particular attention occurred in the large state of Pennsylvania where the incumbent Republican senator, Boies Penrose, sought a third term. A fat, toad-like figure, Penrose had begun public life as a reformer but soon changed into a conservative, high-tariff icon. To many Progressives

Boies Penrose.
A conservative Republican, Boies Penrose easily defeated Gifford Pinchot and A. Mitchell Palmer to retain his Senate seat in 1914. Courtesy of the Library of Congress.

he represented all that was corrupt about the existing political system. Based on the vote in 1912 for Roosevelt and his Washington Party (the name the Progressives used in the state that year), Penrose seemed vulnerable. Gifford Pinchot, the former chief forester of the United States and friend of Roosevelt, decided to make the race. A. Mitchell Palmer, a Democratic member of Congress, carried the banner of Wilson and his administration.

Penrose enjoyed strong support in a state where, more than any other, the protective tariff was almost a religious doctrine. Before the war began, Penrose said, "The coal miners and mill men who are out of work are sick of Democratic administration. They will vote the Republican ticket." On the stump the previously aloof Penrose proved an effective campaigner, in a manner that surprised his opponents. "Pennsylvania will go Republican on the tariff issue," predicted Penrose after a May campaign trip.[11]

Theodore Roosevelt crisscrossed Pennsylvania for Pinchot and the

Washington/Progressive Party but the glamour and intensity of 1912 had not endured. "Smash Penrose, that is the only way you will ever get decent government in Pennsylvania," Roosevelt thundered, "he is the enemy and not the friend of the people."[12] The crowds were large and enthusiastic, but for Roosevelt and his star power, not for Pinchot.

Pinchot and Palmer campaigned within the state, too, but it was a Republican year in a high-tariff state. Pinchot went so far as to endorse the protective policy, but the conservationist was an unlikely champion of that traditional Republican cause. Pinchot worked hard but the death of his mother and his own illness held him back. In the end none of it mattered. Penrose won in a landslide with 520,000 votes to 269,000 for Pinchot and 266,000 for Palmer. Pinchot blamed "a frightened vote, blindly seeking to secure prosperity."[13] Theodore Roosevelt agreed. "The wageworkers in Pennsylvania as elsewhere simply took the ground that they wanted prosperity and were not concerned as to equity in dividing prosperity."[14] The substantive content of Roosevelt's progressivism, so powerful in 1912 when times were good, and his abstract reform programs, gave way to the more urgent need of workers for actual gains in their income. The repudiation of Roosevelt's reforms lifted Republican hopes that politics was returning to normal. Despite the war, GOP stalwarts expected that the familiar themes of the tariff and Democratic threats to prosperity would once again prevail in 1916.

Because of its large bloc of electoral votes in the future 1916 race, and because it was Theodore Roosevelt's home state, the 1914 contest in New York attracted wide attention. The resurgent Republicans, sensing victory, had selected the district attorney of New York County, Charles Seymour Whitman, to run against the Democratic incumbent, Martin S. Glynn. Identified with the Democratic organization of Tammany Hall and its leader, Charles F. Murphy, Glynn had succeeded William Sulzer, elected in 1912, who had been impeached and convicted in 1913 after he broke away from Murphy and Tammany.

Whitman was forty-six in 1914. He had gained fame for prosecuting policeman Charles Becker for the murder of gambler-mobster Herman Rosenthal in one of the most high-profile trials of the day. The boss of the Republicans in New York, William A. Barnes of Albany, had largely orchestrated the nomination of Whitman. Thus the Republican gubernatorial choice represented to Theodore Roosevelt all that was wrong with politics as usual. "If Whitman would, by his action, show he was the right type of man, we could, with propriety, get behind him in a nonpartisan movement to clean up the State. Unfortunately, he has shown that he is the wrong type of man," Roosevelt concluded.[15]

At first the Progressives in New York looked to Roosevelt to lead their ticket in the state race. Such a prospect had little appeal to the former president. He had held the office as a young man in 1899–1900 when all the political world seemed open to him. Still recovering from his Brazilian ordeal, he saw nothing for his own national interests from what seemed likely to be a losing race for an office he no longer coveted. Such a candidacy would also tie him to New York State and limit his ability to aid Progressives in electoral battles across the nation.

So Roosevelt floated a strange scheme that he hoped would maximize the votes of moderate Republicans and his Progressive followers. He supported a Republican backer of the direct primary, Harvey D. Hinman, as an alternative to Whitman. Roosevelt called him an "excellent up-state Republican" and suggested that New York Progressives nominate him as part of an anti-boss campaign. Progressives in the state recoiled at the idea. One Republican termed Hinman "very much in the nature of a pin head' whose only issue was the idea of a direct primary.[16]

An assassination attempt in Wisconsin in mid-October 1912 left Roosevelt hospitalized and then recuperating. As a result, he could not campaign in New York as he planned. Roosevelt believed, "I must arrange to make my main fight in New York this year."[17] However, the Hinman option backfired on the Progressive leader. After a month of public discussion, Hinman reaffirmed his commitment to the Republicans and his unwillingness to fuse with the Progressives. The outcome made Roosevelt look foolish. Hinman's statement left Roosevelt with no place to go but back to the enfeebled Progressive Party and its very long-shot gubernatorial candidate, Frederick W. Davenport. Roosevelt campaigned hard for Davenport with familiar anti-bossism themes in what proved to be a doomed cause. When the voters spoke, Whitman easily defeated Glynn with Davenport running fourth behind the major party candidates and the independent candidacy of former governor Sulzer. In the nation's largest state, the Republicans had won, another encouraging sign of potential Republican strength in the East in two years.

Because of New York's large bloc of electoral votes, Whitman was perceived at once as a potential GOP candidate in 1916. Yet, he did not prove an effective or popular leader of the state and his boom faltered before the more attractive claims of Elihu Root and Charles Evans Hughes. In any event, Whitman did not worry the Wilson circle. Should the Republicans nominate him, "I do not think that we would ask for anything much easier," concluded one of Wilson's wealthy friends and contributors.[18] Still, the Democratic chances of carrying New York in 1916 were now problematic.

Disappointed at the New York outcome, his thoughts already turning to the emerging issues of World War I and neutrality, Roosevelt complained that "all of the men who for years have demanded that someone stand out against both Barnes and Murphy supported Barnes and Murphy, one or the other, with ardor and enthusiasm."[19] It was all part of a general trend against the Progressives, especially in the East. The Democrats suffered, too, and their chances seemed at more risk with a presidential election in the offing.

The war continued to pose new political challenges. As a result of the economic disruption that the outbreak of fighting in Europe produced and the resulting decline in customs revenues that ensued, Wilson asked Congress for war taxes to offset the loss of income. Before the implementation of the income tax in 1915, trade revenues were still the major source of government funding.

Wilson went before Congress to ask for internal taxes to bring in an additional $1 million. The southern-dominated House brought out a bill whose provisions fell most heavily on taxpayers in northern and midwestern states. It was the beginning of sectional policymaking that would often reappear over the next four years. In response the Republicans began using issues left over from the Civil War to arouse their constituents, claiming that the South was once again out to dominate the North and its people. Observers concluded that the Republicans had reverted to what were known as "bloody shirt" tactics (as when GOP orators had held up allegedly bloody Union tunics and urged listeners to vote as they had once shot). It was still a powerful appeal in certain parts of the North. The sectional appeal also reflected the perennial Republican belief that at bottom there were elements of residual treason within the Democratic Party and its new leader. They would display the bloody shirt as another reason for northern voters to oust Wilson from power.

For the Republicans in Congress the war tax bill came as a political gift. House members of that party argued that "the war in Europe is a feeble excuse for the decline in revenue, even when offered by the President of the United States." Another Republican lawmaker said that "it would be unfair for me to exult as a political proposition at these funeral exercises of the Democratic party."[20]

The war tax bill became a major issue in a significant senatorial race in Illinois where incumbent Republican Lawrence Y. Sherman was facing off against the Democratic candidate and longtime party leader Roger Sullivan. Notorious as a political "boss," Sullivan failed to achieve a presidential endorsement because of his conservatism. Theodore Roosevelt supported the third man in the contest, Raymond Robins, who was running as the Progressive candidate. Sherman, who had supported Roosevelt for the GOP nomination in 1912 but had not bolted, attacked the former president as inconsistent in his politics, calling him "the spoiled child of the political nursery." Sherman argued that the Democrats had betrayed the interests of farmers in the Underwood Tariff and that made prosperity "a mighty big issue in Illinois." Sherman and his colleagues toured the state in a train dubbed "The Prosperity Special." Politicians of both parties agreed that Sherman had forged ahead of Sullivan in the autumn of 1914 and that the Republican assault against the war tax was biting against the Democrats, providing more reason for GOP optimism as the political landscape tilted their way in states they had to have for 1916.[21]

A familiar face enlivened the Illinois campaign. Joseph "Uncle Joe" Cannon, the former Speaker of the House and the embodiment of Republican conservatism, had decided to seek his old seat for what would be his twenty-second term. He continued to insist that "the republican party has ever been and is now a progressive party but it stands for progress." In his campaign announcement, Cannon proclaimed: "we are trying Wilson's democratic policy. If you like it choose a democratic house in November. If you don't like it return a republican house that will tie the hands of the president in dictating destructive legislation."[22]

As the congressional elections proceeded, a consensus emerged about the impact of the conflict on the voters. "The war is undoubtedly helping the Democrats," wrote Elihu Root, "because it distracts people's attention from the causes of the dissatisfaction with the Democratic administration which prevailed very widely."[23] The editors of a leading newspaper reached a similar conclusion. "The whole political situation has changed" because of the European war. The Democratic response of standing behind the president had removed the cutting edge from the Republican momentum that had seemed so powerful for so long. "If the Democrats retain control of the next Congress it will be because of the popularity of the president."[24] The Republicans believed that they deserved a landslide on the scale of 1894, which the war was taking away.

When the votes were tabulated, the political alignment had shuddered but the Democratic hold on power continued. Nineteen fourteen did not turn out to be 1894 again. The GOP gained fifty-eight seats in the House and cut the huge Democratic majority of 1912 down to a dozen seats. Yet the Democrats also picked up five Senate seats to increase their margin in the upper house to 55 to 40. Three of their victories came in Wisconsin, South Dakota, and California, a portent of growing Democratic strength in the West that would be evident two years later. Sherman won in Illinois and would prove a partisan nuisance to Wilson and the Democrats in the 1916 contest. All in all, life would be more difficult for President Woodrow Wilson but not impossible.

The Republicans made the most in public of their electoral success. They regarded their victories in such large states as New York, Illinois, and Pennsylvania as indicators of their chances of ousting Wilson in 1916. The triumph of Warren G. Harding in Ohio where he rolled up a plurality of over 100,000 votes based on an inclusive campaign seemed a portent of things to come and a harbinger of a national Republican victory two years later on the scale of McKinley's triumph in 1896, the touchstone among Republicans for their electoral supremacy.

Electing Republican governors in these states was taken as another sign of the resurgence of the Grand Old Party. Newspaper stories announced that the party would prevail on the basis of a presidential campaign whose twin themes would be a strong national defense and tariff protection. To win, the party had only to select an attractive presidential candidate to oppose the hated Wilson. Newspapers speculated about likely Republican contenders.

Charles D. Hilles, the holdover chair of the Republican National Committee from the Taft administration, predicted "that the Republican party will return to power in 1916." Furthermore "the issue in 1916 will be squarely on the tariff and on the legislation of the Democratic party." Labor and business would unite to overthrow Wilson and his party. "The public has sickened of the nostrums and panaceas exploited in the past few years," Hilles concluded. Two decades after William McKinley had led the Grand Old Party to the White House, Republican leaders did not expect the war to stand in the way of the economic issue that would result in another election victory along the lines of 1896.[25]

The big losers in the 1914 contests were Theodore Roosevelt and the dwindling remnants of his Progressive Party. Without the stimulus of a presidential election and even with Roosevelt's energetic campaign, the third party almost disappeared. Their congressional delegation in the House was cut in half to nine and only one Progressive member remained in the Senate. Such party stalwarts as former secretary of the interior under Roosevelt, James R. Garfield, and former senator Albert J. Beveridge in Indiana made poor showings in gubernatorial races in their states. The reelection of Hiram Johnson as governor of California was the lone bright spot. "East of Indiana," wrote a disappointed Roosevelt, "it would be mere silliness and fruitful of nothing except a trifle or mischief to endeavor at present to continue action along Progressive lines exactly as we have done."[26] In the West, Roosevelt concluded, "the party must keep up." Because the country "was sick and tired of reform," the best the Progressives could do was to exist only on a state-by-state basis.[27] It was a long way from the optimism of the third party in 1912.

The outbreak of the war had traumatized Roosevelt in both a personal and professional sense, and he focused his energies more and more on foreign policy. It was a trick of fate that denied him the large role in world affairs and gave the task to, in his mind, the unqualified and timid Woodrow Wilson. Roosevelt believed that the incumbent was a physical coward (a damning condition for Roosevelt) who was "entirely cold-blooded and selfish."[28] Had Roosevelt been in office he would have reacted against German aggression in Belgium with decisive action, including sending American forces to Europe, which in his mind could have deterred Berlin. The crucial thing was to get back to the White House, and for the moment the Progressive Party, a shadow of the enthusiasm of 1912, seemed the best vehicle to get him back to the center of American power.

As the American neutrality period progressed, however, Roosevelt came to see the Republicans as the only viable way he could regain the presidency. The Progressive Party, launched to deprive Taft of the White House, might be a diversion against the Wilson administration that Roosevelt now detested. The former president's political judgment was less astute since he had departed from the White House. His course in 1915–1916 would be that of a man obsessed with returning to the White House so he might play a role in the world crisis.

Within the Wilson administration, the election results elicited sighs of relief that the Democrats had escaped a repudiating disaster at the hands of the voters. The Democrats had long respected the electoral abilities of the Republican campaign apparatus that had defeated them so often since the mid-1890s. Now in what had become a straight two-party contest outside of the South, the Democrats had confronted their rivals and had not been ousted from Congress.

President Wilson himself, though, felt the party's losses personally. He told Edward M. House, his closest confidant, that "it seemed hardly worthwhile to work as hard as he had worked during the past two years and to have it so scantily appreciated." When House told him that he was not running and Americans had cast ballots for others, Wilson countered: "People are not so stupid not to know that to vote against a democratic ticket is to vote indirectly against me."[29]

The outcome of the 1914 elections occurred at a time when Wilson was considering the future direction of his presidency. Not at all a radical politician, the president noted as any leader would the loss of support for political reform that was so evident during 1914. As a Missouri Republican noted, "all over the country there is a feeling that the so-called sandbagging [anti-corporate] legislation should cease."[30]

To get out in front of the skepticism about further reforms and to court the business community for which he had an *innate* respect, Wilson sent out signals that he was not a foe of enterprise in an effort to establish more fruitful connections with corporate leaders. It was something of a futile endeavor since the business leaders he spoke with and wrote to were not going to abandon their Republican allegiance no matter what the president told them. So in the middle of the 1914 campaign, Wilson said in his letter to Representative Underwood that "it is our purpose to destroy monopoly and maintain competition as the only effectual instrument of business liberty." He did not, however, give explicit assurances that he would defer to business in the future.[31]

Wilson sought to counter the impression of an antibusiness sentiment in the White House, exemplified in the campaign to pass the Federal Trade Commission in the fall of 1914, by openly courting corporate leaders as the elections neared. Wilson wrote a public letter (a missive designed to be released to the press by its very nature) on behalf of A. Mitchell Palmer in which he said that "the reconstructive legislation which for the last two decades the opinion of the country had demanded and which the political parties of the country have vied with each other in promising have been enacted."[32]

In an interview with reporter (and future biographer) Ray Stannard Baker on September 7, Wilson opined "that he had nearly reached the end of his economic program as outlined in the campaign and Democratic platform"; only issues of the merchant marine and conservation needed to be addressed.[33] In addition, the day after the election, the *Washington Post* reported that given "a rebuke at the polls, there would be no further effort to enact laws aimed at business, and the industries of the country would be given a season of rest."[34]

The annual message that Wilson delivered to Congress on December 8, 1914, did not in its original version contain any soothing language about the business community. Joe Tumulty, after discussing the proposed message with the president, said, "Your failure to mention business legislation and the completion of our programme regarding it, will lead to suspicion and doubt."[35]

In response to Tumulty's suggestion, Wilson told the lawmakers that "the program with regard to the regulation of business is now virtually complete." The president added that "the road at last lies clear and firm before business." The editors of the *New York Times* agreed with the president's posture. "The cudgeling of corporations is no longer profitable politically, the country has set its face against it."[36]

To drive the point home, Wilson turned to another of his public letters, this time to Secretary of the Treasury William G. McAdoo, on November 17. The president pointed to the issues of the first decade of the century—the control of business, the need to lower the tariff, and the creation of the Federal Reserve system—and proclaimed that "the legislation of the last year and a half has in very large measure done away with those things." He asserted that "the future is clear and bright with the promise of best things" and he looked forward to "a time of healing because of just dealing." There would be "a new spirit, a new enthusiasm, a new cordiality of spirited co-operation."[37]

The president's jaunty conclusion that the main tasks for reform had been accomplished and that business need not fear for the future did not sit well among Progressives. The editors of the new reformist journal *The New Republic* said that the letter showed Wilson had "utterly misconceived the meaning and task of American progressivism." The president was, they concluded, "a dangerous and unsound thinker upon contemporary political and social problems."[38]

Historians (following Wilson biographer Arthur Link) have noted the disaffection that the letter to McAdoo created among Wilson's supporters to his left. Less often remarked is that it did not assuage fears among business leaders on the right, either. Tariff supporters in Pennsylvania sent public letters to the White House questioning whether prosperity had in fact returned and spoke of "wrecks all about us in the iron and steel mills" and asked Wilson to revisit the Underwood Tariff.[39] Nothing Wilson did to reassure business could undermine the fixed Republican disdain for him and his party.

As Congress returned for a lame-duck session in December 1914–March 1915, two issues arising from the war sharpened divisions between Wilson and his enemies. The first, over the state of the nation's defenses, emerged when Congress came back into session in December. Representative Augustus Peabody Gardner raised the question of military preparedness and argued in a sensational statement in October 1914 that the United States was "totally unprepared for war." He called for a commission to examine how well prepared the nation was.[40] Republican newspapers reported his allegations in banner headlines. President Wilson was unimpressed. He termed what Gardner proposed only a "good mental exercise" and concluded that "talk of this sort has been going on ever since he was a boy of ten."[41]

Gardner and Lodge introduced resolutions to probe the nation's defenses as soon as Congress met on December 7. Their actions mixed conviction and politics. Newspapers had already indicated that national defense would accompany tariff protection as a GOP theme in 1916. Gardner and Lodge were also genuinely concerned whether the nation could fight effectively in case of a conflict and that a strong military would help the United States remain at peace. If President Wilson looked bad in the process, it was no more than what a feckless Democrat deserved.[42]

The White House did not take Gardner seriously and the Wilson administration brushed him aside. In his State of the Union address, Wilson said that "this is a time above all others when we should wish and resolve to keep our strength by self-possession, our influence by preserving our ancient principles of action." There was no need to build up the army. Overall "we shall not alter our attitude toward it because some amongst us are nervous and excited."[43]

Wilson exercised his control of the military establishment to prevent its leaders from echoing GOP charges and he persuaded Democratic leaders in Congress to keep defense appropriations down. Public opinion supported the president and the issue stalled for the remainder of the year and into 1915. Lodge and Gardner had been blocked. Gardner had warned that "I am very much afraid that the president means to lay the cold hand of death upon the world movement" and so for the moment it proved. A Republican editor told Roosevelt that the issue was "whether ours shall continue to be a government of laws or a government of grape juice dispensed by molly coddles."[44] Again, Wilson acted in a manner to heighten Republican distrust of his conduct.

In his annual message, Wilson set off an even more bitter political fight with his legislation that the United States purchase German ships that had been caught in American harbors at the beginning of the war and could not return home without being intercepted by the British navy. The money would be paid to the German government and the ships would be added to the merchant marine. The initiative outraged Republican senators and an intense battle ensued in the upper house in the winter of 1915. More than any other single event of Wilson's first term, the ship purchase controversy foreshadowed the ideological struggle the 1916 election would become.

There was much in the bill to provoke Republican opposition. The money would go to Germany, an unneutral act. The scheme could bring on a confrontation with Britain and France if those countries treated the purchased ships as belligerent vessels. But the greatest ideological objection was to the very character of what Wilson and McAdoo sought to do. "It means a departure on the lines of government more important and more fateful in its results than any act passed by this Congress since I became a member," said Elihu Root.[45] A British observer found Republican opposition fascinating. "Isn't it astonishing that the two great political parties in America exchange positions? Root who is a great leader of the party of protection and paternalism is now the leader of the opposition to state socialism, while Wilson, the successor of Jefferson and Cleveland, both as President & leader of the party of individualism, has become the champion of a state owned merchant marine."[46]

Suspicion about the motives of the opposing sides added to the intensity of the mutual ill feelings. Republicans charged that Secretary McAdoo was involved with the banking firm of Kuhn, Loeb in pushing for the ship purchase because of ships owned by a brother of a member of the firm, Paul Warburg. The charge came to nothing but the Wilson administration encountered another public allegation of scandal like the one that had been made against the president over Panama Canal tolls.[47] Republicans questioned the honesty of the president and his administration.

On the Republican side, members further bristled when the White

House appointed the brother of a Republican senator to a postmastership in Iowa in what seemed on its face to be a transparent attempt to sway a wavering vote. Senators called it "a brutal disregard to decency" which Henry Cabot Lodge had "never seen surpassed." Lodge told Roosevelt "there is a coarse cynicism about such an act as this."[48]

In the middle of the ship purchase fight Wilson decided to attack his partisan enemies as well as Senate Democrats who had reservations about the bill. He spoke at Indianapolis on January 8, 1915, celebrating the birthday of Democratic icon Andrew Jackson. It was the most political address of his first term up to that time and it instilled in Republicans a permanent sense of grievance. "The Republican party is still a covert and a refuge for those who are afraid, who want to consult their grandfathers about everything," the president alleged. In fact, Wilson said Republicans had "not known how to do anything except sit on the lid." He criticized Democrats who opposed him on the ship purchase bill and once again sought to reassure business leaders about his policies. He made some snide remarks about educating uninstructed Republicans on the tariff "though I have not always taught in the primary grade." The GOP, he contended, did not "seem to have any great emotions. They seem to think a lot of things, old things, but they do not seem to have any enthusiasm about anything."[49]

It was a new experience for the Republicans to be the target of presidential twitting and they did not like it. The attack of the President on the minority of the Senate was "unfair, undignified and inexcusable," said Jacob H. Gallinger, Republican from New Hampshire. For Reed Smoot of Utah it proved the charge "that he is seeking to concentrate in himself all the powers of the three coordinate branches of the government."[50] Henry Cabot Lodge articulated Republican anger in a letter to his old friend Roosevelt. "The whole speech was not only angry, but cheap and the natural cheapness of the man had come out. I live in hopes that he will be found out by the people of the United States for what he really is."[51]

Wilson reciprocated Lodge's feelings. Of Lodge and Root, who had supported him in the Panama Canal tolls battle in the winter of 1914, he wrote to a friend: "it is a very grim business in which they will give no quarter and in which, so far as I am concerned, they will receive none."[52] It was in this period that Lodge expressed his personal emotions of hatred toward the president. For Lodge, Taft, Root, and even more for Roosevelt, the defeat of Wilson in 1916 was now not just a political aim. It became a moral crusade to be pursued and fought by every means at hand. Personal rumors about Wilson's character and alleged marital infidelity to his first wife circulated among Republicans and were given ready credence. The bitterness and rancor of the upcoming presidential contest was the legacy of the 1914 election and what followed in the lame-duck session of 1914–1915.

3

THE REPUBLICAN FIELD

The outcome of the 1914 elections convinced the Republicans that they would win the White House in 1916 and do so with comparative ease. The commissioner of internal revenue, a North Carolina Democrat named William H. Osborn, wrote in his diary on December 27, 1914, that "I have never seen the Republicans more jubilant than they are now; they confidently expect to win in 1916." The situation did not change during the ensuing winter. "Here in the East," wrote a Republican journalist in April 1915, "political opinion is rapidly settling down to a confident—perhaps over-confident—feeling that another 1896 is ahead of us so far as Republican prospects go."[1]

In light of the virtual certainty that the Republicans would prevail, all that was needed to achieve the inevitable victory was to find the proper candidate to advance the goals of tariff protection and national defense, and the hated Wilson would be swept away on a righteous tide of voter protest. The natural order of American politics, with Republicans in power, would be restored, the tariff could then be raised to proper levels, and all would be well again. In the process President Wilson would be unmasked as the opportunist that most Republicans believed him to be and the words of his critics vindicated. GOP members yearned for such a result.

The trick, of course, was to find just the right candidate who could fulfill the passionate expectations that dominated the Republicans as the election of 1916 approached. The successful aspirant must be able to induce the shrinking remnant of the Progressive Party back into the fold while at the same time retaining the allegiance of the party's conservative base. As the war entered 1915, it was also becoming clear that a presidential candidate would have to be firm enough on neutrality issues toward Germany to hold the support of the pro-Allied East while being sufficiently neutral to avoid alienating German Americans and midwestern Republicans, who above all else sought to keep out of the European war.

For the first time since 1896 there was not a clear, designated hopeful who was likely to emerge from the Republican selection process as the winner of the prize. The absence of an evident front-runner made Republicans nervous as the months of 1915 went by. The party, said one observer, "must have a candidate on whom divergent factions can unite: who will neither terrify the conservatives nor disgust the radical."[2] Surely the party would not miss its opportunity, so tantalizingly close, to rid the nation of Woodrow Wilson.

Some famous names could be quickly ruled out. There was no sentiment for another race from the 1912 nominee, William Howard Taft. Happy as a professor teaching law at Yale College in New Haven, Connecticut, Taft knew that his electoral relations with the Republican Party were over. "I am not in the field at all, and do not expect to be. I am out of politics, and glad to be out," Taft wrote in December 1914. He hoped that the election of a Republican president might open the way for his selection as Chief Justice of the United States, a position he had long coveted. A second priority was Taft's intention of doing everything that he could to prevent Theodore Roosevelt from being the Republican nominee in 1916. According to Taft, Roosevelt did not know "the abysmal depths that he has reached in the opinion of the men who are likely to control the Republican Convention and Republican politics in the next presidential campaign."[3]

As for Roosevelt himself, he told colleagues after the Progressive debacle in the 1914 elections, "I cannot see clearly as to what the future will be." Therefore he thought it best "that I shall avoid political speechmaking or any appearance of taking an active part in the party politics of the day." The Progressive executive committee met in Chicago on December 2, 1914, without Roosevelt present, and agreed in what seemed a futile gesture that the party would continue. Roosevelt also pulled away from the perceived radicalism of the Pinchot brothers. While he prepared to defend himself in the case of the libel suit that William A.

Barnes had filed against him, his disgust with Wilson and Secretary of State William Jennings Bryan had become boundless. "Our foreign affairs were managed badly under Taft," he wrote, "but they have never been managed quite as badly as they are under Messrs Wilson and Bryan and [Josephus] Daniels."[4]

Throughout 1915 Roosevelt intensified his rhetoric in his attacks on the White House over foreign policy. He had been neutral at the outset of the fighting, but soon became convinced of the validity of atrocity charges against Germany for its treatment of Belgium, and he decided that Berlin had been the aggressor and was a potential threat to the United States.[5] In the event that Germany attacked, the United States would need to strengthen its military defenses. Roosevelt joined the preparedness crusade of the National Security League and General Leonard Wood. He also advocated a firmer policy toward Mexico and the continuing attacks on American citizens there. A newspaper headline well summed up how Roosevelt came across to the public in these months: "Roosevelt for War."[6] If by chance the Republicans should select Roosevelt as their nominee, they would be embracing a chief executive who would take the nation into war on the Allied side. Along with the lingering resentments about his conduct in 1912 among Republican regulars, Roosevelt promised likely defeat for the GOP in a contest with Wilson and the Democrats.

Impressions of Roosevelt's bellicosity strengthened as 1915 unfolded. After the *Lusitania* sinking, Roosevelt denounced the event and the American loss of life as piracy "on a vaster scale of murder than any old-time pirate ever practiced." When another such incident occurred in the sinking of the *Arabic*, Roosevelt sought a diplomatic rupture with Germany, a prelude to war.[7]

With Roosevelt having so many weaknesses, eastern Republicans who sought a more pro-Allied, aggressive foreign policy looked to former senator Elihu Root as their potential leader. William A. Barnes and the Republican hierarchy in New York advanced Root's claims. Root was strongly anti-German in his feelings about the war and thought the United States should have entered the conflict after the sinking of the *Lusitania*. He was committed to preparedness and his warlike feelings would have been as anathema to the Middle West as Roosevelt's were.[8]

Yet the weaknesses that had prevented Root from being Roosevelt's choice to succeed him in 1908 still operated to limit the former senator's appeal. Root was seventy-one in 1915, old for a presidential candidate, and the memories of his past as a lawyer for corporations cast a shadow over his distinguished record as secretary of war and secretary of state under McKinley and Roosevelt. For the more committed Progressives, Root was also still the man who had helped Taft, in their minds, steal the nomination from Roosevelt in 1912 by chairing the Republican National Convention. Beyond that, in June 1915 Root told Taft "that he hated to meet people and could not stand the Presidency." Root would be a favorite son for New York Republicans in a strategy called "Roosting on Root" until they could find a better alternative.[9]

With their past leaders ruled out for various reasons, Republicans explored the prospects of some fresh faces in 1915. One potential aspirant was Ambassador to France Myron T. Herrick. He had been a friend and ally of William McKinley in Ohio politics.[10] After being elected governor of Ohio in 1903, he was talked of as a coming Republican with national ambitions. Then he stumbled with an unexpected reelection loss in 1903 when Ohio voters were in an anti-bossism mood. He remained a large figure whose name was often mentioned for cabinet posts in the Roosevelt and Taft presidencies.[11]

Taft appointed Herrick as ambassador to France in 1912. Herrick sent in his resignation to president-elect Wilson in February 1913. The Wilson administration encountered difficulty in finding a deserving and well-heeled Democrat to take up the duties of the Paris post. By mid-summer 1914 William Graves Sharp, a wealthy Democratic contributor, had been confirmed as Herrick's replacement and sailed for France to become ambassador in early August.[12]

By that time World War I had begun, and Herrick was dealing with the plight of tens of thousands of Americans displaced and stranded by the fighting. He did so with energy and efficiency and Ambassador Sharp stood aside and "voluntarily refrained from taking over the affairs of the embassy because he realizes that Herrick should not be relieved at such a critical juncture."[13] Herrick's performance endeared him to his French hosts.

In late November Herrick was on his way home, and Sharp had taken over. Republicans believed that Wilson had replaced Herrick for partisan purposes and his recall was not justified. It was a popular and recurrent talking point within the GOP and it led to discussion in early 1915 of Herrick as a presidential possibility. As Henry Cabot Lodge told him, "you are the logical candidate and you can be elected hands down. You have been absent nearly three years and fortunately you have not been

Myron Herrick.
Ambassador to France under Presidents Taft and Wilson, Herrick was thought of as a possible presidential candidate in 1915. Courtesy of the Library of Congress.

mixed up in all the rows of 1912. Everybody knows you and everybody is for you."[14]

Herrick talk was prevalent in the early months of 1915. "Republican lightning might flash further and strike worse," concluded the nation's main Democratic paper, the *New York World*.[15] Yet, despite the popularity of Herrick among Republicans, and his plan to make rural credits legislation the center of his appeal, his candidacy did not take off. Herrick thought his business past was a liability for his chances. By early 1916 he announced his candidacy in Ohio to oppose incumbent Democratic senator Atlee Pomerene in Ohio and thus abandoned any presidential ambitions.

New England offered its own choice in the candidacy of Senator John Wingate Weeks of Massachusetts. He had attended the Naval Academy and served several years in the navy before becoming a banker. He was elected to the House in 1905 and Speaker Cannon put him on the Agriculture Committee.[16] On the major issues of the day, Weeks was a conservative Republican, in favor of the protective tariff, skeptical of government regulation, and pro-preparedness. In April 1910 he wrote that "My own judgement is that the Payne-Aldrich bill is an excellent bill, and that, relatively speaking, Massachusetts will never get a better one."[17] He had voted for Canadian Reciprocity in 1911, but feared that "the next point of attack will be on the rates of duty on our manufacturing industries."[18]

Since he came from a state and region that was heavily Republican, Weeks needed to show that he had an appeal beyond the borders of New England. A western swing for speech making before party members in June 1915 pleased his supporters but dismayed Progressives when he attacked woman suffrage and prohibition. Theodore Roosevelt heard these complaints. "I hear from the West that Weeks made a very bad impression by his speeches out there. They were treated as reactionary and standpat."[19]

In his public appearances, Weeks had called the Federal Trade Commission "the outgrowth of fevered minds." He denounced Wilson's Mexican policy. "'Watchful waiting' has been tried for two years now, and matters are worse than ever before. How do you think people will vote after what they have seen and heard?" In Portland, Oregon, he said: "The return of the Republican party to power is sure. If the elections were held tomorrow, the Republicans would sweep the country."[20]

By the start of 1916, Weeks had become fixed as a favorite son of

John W. Weeks. A conservative Republican from Massachusetts, Weeks made a run for the GOP nomination in 1915–1916, but ended up as only a regional favorite son. Courtesy of the Library of Congress.

Massachusetts and no more than that. A Washington reporter said in February that "the cagey old owls are not as strong for Weeks as some would have us believe.[21] As the convention approached in May 1916, another reporter from the Bay State predicted that "Senator Weeks will receive the votes of twenty-five delegates at least on the first ballot on condition that a complimentary endorsement is all that he asks as a free will offering."[22] The Weeks boom faltered as the prospects of Charles Evans Hughes improved during the spring of 1916.

The existing Republican field contained some other long shots. From Iowa, Senator Albert B. Cummins, who a decade earlier had seemed radical but was now moving toward conservatism, controlled his state's delegation but had little support elsewhere.[23] In February 1916 Senator Robert M. La Follette of Wisconsin announced his presidential candidacy on an antiwar platform. He, too, had his state's delegation in his pocket but scant appeal beyond its borders.[24] There was talk about the eloquent Idaho senator William E. Borah, but his state was too small and too remote to make him a credible electoral alternative. Senator Lawrence Yates Sherman had White House ambitions, but it was not certain he could control the Illinois delegation.[25] Charles W. Fairbanks of Indiana, vice president under Roosevelt, and one of those figures who was renowned for his dullness, hoped to do better than he had done in 1908 but was essentially only one of the favorite sons.[26]

The Republicans needed a savior and throughout 1915 and into 1916 the chances of one man improved as the Republicans looked with great longing at an unblemished candidate, free from the internecine battles of 1912, who could defeat the hated Wilson and lead the Grand Old Party back to the White House. In the minds of many Republicans the name of Justice Charles Evans Hughes stood before them, like an oasis in a political desert, as the ideal candidate to confront the incumbent and send him to the defeat he deserved. Safe in the chambers of the Supreme Court since his appointment to the bench in 1910 by President Taft, Hughes had said nothing on the issues of the day, had stayed out of the imbroglio of 1912, and yet seemed the perfect foil to Woodrow Wilson.

Charles Evans Hughes is one of the most enigmatic figures in American politics in the Progressive Era. The standard biography, a two-volume tome published in 1951, does not get into the complexities of Hughes's career. Subsequent works on his years as governor reveal a more nuanced person and explain why professional politicians in New York did not like the state's chief executive between 1907 and 1910. Hughes is more of an historical icon than a full-blooded individual. Understanding his strengths and weaknesses is crucial to grasping why he became the Republican nominee in 1916 and then why he lost.[27]

Hughes was born in 1862, the son of a Baptist clergyman in New York State. From an early age he displayed the intellectual brilliance that carried him through Brown University and Columbia Law School with distinction. He was a Republican from his youth but that partisanship faded in adult life. He cheered for Rutherford B. Hayes in 1876 and

Charles Evans Hughes. Elected as governor of New York in 1906, Hughes went on to the U.S. Supreme Court in 1910. Republicans saw him as the way to beat their hated enemy, Woodrow Wilson. Courtesy of the Library of Congress.

campaigned for James A. Garfield in 1880. As he recalled, "We organized a Garfield battalion and with caps, capes, banners and torches, we marched in Providence, Bristol, and Boston, returning late at night after a heavy dose of campaign oratory."[28] The militarized practices of Hughes's first presidential campaign would be a dim memory when he sought the White House thirty-six years later.

Hughes first came to public view in New York in 1905 when he was asked to be counsel for a probe into the utilities industry and then requested to take a similar role into corrupt practices in the powerful insurance business. His relentless, understated questioning style exposed the unsavory side of this lucrative trade. So successful was Hughes in exposing corporate wrong-doing that the Republicans offered him the nomination for mayor of New York City in 1905. He refused because he did not want to get into local politics at that time He was seen as a coming man among Republicans and they viewed him as a potential governor as well. That option soon became a real one for Hughes.

After the Democrats nominated the millionaire publisher William Randolph Hearst for governor in 1906, the Republicans were faced with what they perceived to be a radical challenge to their grip on power. A New York Republican told President Roosevelt in July 1906 that "it will not do to underestimate Hearst's strength this year. He will, of course cut into the Democratic vote but his inroad in our own vote last year [when Hearst ran for mayor of New York City and lost] should not be underestimated."[29]

Roosevelt looked to Hughes to win the state house for the Republicans. "[Benjamin B.] Odell and [Thomas Collier] Platt want Hughes," Roosevelt wrote, "and upon my word I am not at all certain but that it would be well to nominate him." The professionals had little idea of Hughes and what kind of governor he would be, but they yielded to White House pressure and went along with Roosevelt.[30]

The Hearst-Hughes campaign was a heated one. The new GOP candidate attacked Hearst and promised decent government. Hughes played down partisanship, as did the Republicans in general, and focused his criticism on Hearst's sordid reputation. The two men differed, for example, on whether they had fully paid their state taxes. At least one Republican viewing the campaign anticipated an allegation that would be made against Hughes ten years later. "His campaign has not at any time, I think, risen above the level of personal criticism, and you and I know that this is not a very firm basis upon which to place a political campaign."[31]

The key moment in the race did not involve Hughes. Worried about the chances of a Hearst victory, Roosevelt deployed his secretary of state. As Elihu Root told a conservative senator on October 30, 1906, "I am just about going over to New York to make speech concerning our New York La Follette, commonly called Hearst."[32] In Utica, with the contest still up in the air, Root told his audience that in the aftermath of President McKinley's death, President Roosevelt had denounced "the reckless utterances of those who, on the stump and in the public press, appeal to the dark and evil spirits of malice and greed, envy and sullen hatred."

When Roosevelt wrote those words, said Root, "he had Mr. Hearst specifically in mind and I say by his authority that what he thought of Mr. Hearst then he thinks of Mr. Hearst now."[33] The Republicans circulated the Root speech widely over the weekend before the election and what Root said was believed to have carried Hughes to his 58,000-vote triumph over Hearst.[34] The future chief justice did not refer to Root's comment in his autobiographical notes.

In Albany, Hughes proved an effective, activist governor whose stance pleased the voters more than it did the professional politicians. His secretary wrote "the local bosses find it very hard to learn the lesson that political responsibility must be divorced from financial considerations."[35] As a result, the professionals felt that Hughes, who had depended on their support for his election, now treated them as unworthy pariahs. One of his signal accomplishments was a measure to outlaw gambling at horse race tracks. His anti-bossism rhetoric and willingness to appeal over the heads of politicians to the voters themselves became a touchstone of the Hughes political style. The Republican boss in New York, William A. Barnes, complained to Elihu Root in January 1909 that "one must agree with the Governor in every particular, or be rated a 'crook.'"[36]

Having, at least in his own mind, made Hughes the governor, Theodore Roosevelt expected that the new state executive would look to him for advice and follow the president's suggestions. After all, Roosevelt had once held the same office on his way to the White House. It was not to be as the self-confident Hughes saw no reason to defer to Roosevelt. The president ousted a minor patronage official in upstate New York. The press said that Hughes disapproved of the action. Roosevelt felt betrayed and embarrassed. One did not treat the president in such a cavalier manner. His initial esteem for Hughes never recovered from this incident.[37]

It was natural that as Hughes succeeded in his political tryout in New York affairs, newspaper speculation about a possible presidential race grew in 1907. Since Roosevelt had already decided that Taft should follow him in the White House, the public consideration of a Hughes boom did not sit well with a president already disillusioned with the governor. "The men most hostile to me show a tendency to gather around Hughes," Roosevelt told his son Kermit. "Hughes, a fairly good man (but not a big man) and an inordinately conceited one."[38]

Taft was rolling toward the Republican nomination at the start of 1908 and Hughes posed no real threat to his chances. Rather than precipitate a fight in New York that might endanger carrying the Empire State in the presidential contest, Roosevelt and Taft decided to let New York Republicans send their delegation to the convention pledged to Hughes as a favorite son.

Roosevelt did not take any chances or give the Hughes boom any political air. When Hughes planned to issue a formal declaration of where he stood on national issues, Roosevelt sent to Congress that same day one of his most radical messages. The headlines went to Roosevelt, the inside pages to the New York governor, and the overall benefit accrued to Taft. Roosevelt told a reporter: "If Hughes is going to play the game, he must learn the tricks." It is doubtful that Hughes forgot the episode.[39]

Taft gained the GOP nomination on the first ballot with Hughes a very weak third. Taft offered the vice presidency to Hughes but he turned the place down. "It would be impossible for me in any event to take the nomination for Vice President," Hughes replied to the White House.[40] Soon the question became whether the governor would run for a second term.

If Hughes were to be rejected and some other newcomer placed on the ballot, Republican hopes of carrying New York against Bryan and the Democrats might be in peril, with the possibility of losing the entire election. Much as he disliked Hughes as a politician, Roosevelt decided that Hughes had to be renominated, no matter what the professionals in New York might think. At a meeting with New Yorkers on August 20 at Oyster Bay, "the consensus of opinion was that Hughes although none present liked him" should be renominated.[41]

To mollify his critics, Hughes needed a chance to validate his credentials as a partisan, and an opportunity offered itself just two weeks before the Republican state convention would meet to decide his fate. He was invited to give an address at a Republican rally in Youngstown, Ohio, that would mark the formal start of the GOP campaign for Taft in Ohio. The event would be covered nationally and it would for Hughes be a good indicator of the state of his skill as an articulate voice for classic Republican doctrine.The Hughes speech in Ohio came at an awkward moment for the Republican presidential campaign of William Howard Taft. Running for the third time, William Jennings Bryan and his party were full of hope against Taft, whom they regarded as a weaker candidate than either McKinley or Roosevelt had been. The Taft campaign, under Frank H. Hitchcock, seemed slow in getting started, and no one knew how Taft would perform on the stump. There was unease within the GOP, not that Taft would lose (an unthinkable prospect), but that a harder fight lay ahead than the Republicans had faced for some time.

A large crowd turned out to see Hughes and his fellow orators, Senator Albert J. Beveridge of Indiana (usually a compelling speaker) and a local Ohio politician. The *New-York Tribune*, always a reliably Republican newspaper, called it "the greatest outpouring of Republicans which has marked the opening of a political campaign in the years of Ohio's history."[42] Roosevelt Cabinet members attended along with Ohio worthies and an audience estimated well into the thousands. Hughes spoke after Beveridge and moved his listeners to repeated shouts of approval.

Hughes began his remarks with an avowal of his party's superior claims to hold political power. "The Republican party makes appeal to public confidence as the most important agency for conservation and progress." The Democratic Party, on the other hand, "memorializes the fallacies and unsafe policies we are asked to forget, and it points the way to business uncertainty, and to the impairment of that confidence which is the security of industry and trade."[43]

He derided Bryan's campaign slogan "Shall the People Rule?" as unimpressive when Tammany Hall, the longtime party bastion, carried the Democratic banner in New York. "We may well pause before we permit it, despite its boast of fidelity, to garrison our institutions," an oblique allusion to the perennial Republican suspicion of Democratic legitimacy. He praised Taft's candidacy and invoked the Republican past of McKinley and Roosevelt. "We have got our direction, we have a most precious cargo, and we must have a safe and experienced pilot." Because Bryan had endorsed free silver in 1896 and later government ownership of the railroads in 1906, he could not "be regarded as a safe leader to whom may be confided the great powers of the Presidency merely because these doctrines are omitted from his present platform."[44]

The meat of the speech consisted of his assaults on Bryan's proposed remedies for industrial consolidation and the excesses of big business. He scoffed at the proposal that Bryan advanced to require that firms would have to obtain a federal license to control anything over 25 percent of what they produced. "In a desire to correct the evils of business are we to place an embargo upon honest endeavor whose activities present none of the abuses requiring remedies?" Hughes then asked a number of specific questions about the Bryan business program which, he concluded, "stamps the Democratic program with the fatal stamp of 1896."[45]

Hughes also dismissed Bryan's idea for the guarantee of bank deposits. He proclaimed his own and Republican concern for working men and women in an industrial state such as Ohio. The customary GOP answers of tariff protection and sound money remained the keys to prosperity. "It is not a time for Nostrums," Hughes concluded, "or for the rule of a party which proposes them."[46] According to the accounts in Republican newspapers, the audience was familiar with Hughes and his standing in New York. There were shouted endorsements from the crowd for a second term.

Republicans were overjoyed with what Hughes had said. Taft told Roosevelt of his pleasure with the speech. The reporter for the *New-York Tribune* said that Hughes "handled his subject in so masterful a manner as to create the best possible impression and to inspire every Republican to do his utmost."[47] Hughes was hard-hitting, specific, and to Republicans utterly convincing. So totemic did the Youngstown speech become among Republicans that the party quoted passages from it eight years later in the 1916 campaign textbook as though the voters had only to be reminded of what Hughes had once proclaimed.[48]

Ever since Bryan had burst upon the national scene in 1896 with his "Cross of Gold" speech, Republicans had regarded him as a demagogic mountebank. To see Hughes expose him for what GOP members believed him to be was gratifying. The New York *Sun* said Bryan was great only because of what he had been prevented from doing. For Hughes to say so in a single, compelling speech was "a masterpiece of political analysis, delicate in wit, searching in insight, tremendous in significance."[49]

The speech nailed down Hughes's bona fides as he approached the state convention. More importantly, it implanted the enduring idea among Republicans that Hughes when speaking at his best was a formidable adversary. By 1915 party leaders judged that, if he could dissect the vagaries of Bryan in 1908, what might he do to what Republican leaders deemed in their heart of hearts to be the sophistries of Woodrow Wilson? An ideal Hughes took shape in the minds of his potential backers in 1915–1916. In the whiskered jurist the party would have someone who could go toe-to-toe against Wilson, and not just win, but reveal Wilson for the fraud Republicans knew he was.

The Youngstown speech firmed up Hughes's Republican standing. Buttressed by the heavy endorsement from the White House, Hughes secured the party's 1908 nomination at the state convention to run against the Democratic lieutenant governor, Lewis Chanler. One disgruntled Republican said: "If Hughes were more of a human being, and a little less like a heathen god, he would be much stronger with the people, but he represents the reform idea and therefore his nomination will be exceedingly helpful to our party in New York."[50]

Facing an incumbent, Lewis Chanler tried a bold strategy. To dent the popularity of the governor and shake up the race, he posed ten pointed questions to Hughes in public designed to put him at a disadvantage. Chanler asked: "Are you in favor of a constitutional amendment for the election of United States senators by the people," and "why did you conspicuously omit in your speech of acceptance an expression of your approval of the Republican state platform?"[51]

Hughes made an effective response the next day. To the question about whether he was in favor of the amendment for the direct election of senators, he said: "I am." He denied that he had not referred to the Republican state platform in his acceptance speech. On the whole, Hughes won the exchange and politicians attributed his success to what he had said in rebutting Chanler. Eight years later, reporters remembered that "the complete rout of Chanler was the turning point in that campaign that ended in victory for Hughes."[52] In a match with Wilson, Hughes could bring superior public relations skills or so Republicans presumed. They gave no thought to whether the intervening years on the bench had made Hughes rusty, and in the nature of his unannounced candidacy he could not give any speeches to learn if he was campaign-ready. The Republicans planned to nominate him in a strange blend of memory and desire.

Hughes won reelection though he ran 65,000 votes behind Taft, who easily carried the state against Bryan. In his second term, the governor pursued a program for direct primaries to select party candidates. He sought and received the support of Theodore Roosevelt for his plan in 1910 but failed to persuade the legislature. Republican insiders were predictably opposed and despite the governor's best efforts the direct primary law failed.

But by mid-1910 Hughes's life moved in a different direction. President Taft had been impressed with the intellect of the governor. In March 1910, after the death of Supreme Court Justice David J. Brewer, the president decided to name Hughes to the vacant seat. Hughes was confirmed in May and told the public he would resign as governor in October 1910. Taft hinted that should the post of Chief Justice become open, he would select Hughes. But when Chief Justice Melville Weston Fuller died in July, Taft elevated Justice Edward Douglass White in December.

Had Hughes become Chief Justice, he likely would not have resigned to run for president. Taft preferred an older man rather than have the forty-eight year old Hughes take the place and end any chance that Taft, if not reelected in 1912, might one day succeed White.

Hughes adjusted at once to life as a judge and believed he would end his career on the Court. He was an intelligent and progressive jurist. When the Taft-Roosevelt feud split the party, some voices suggested Hughes as a compromise choice.[53] Hughes declined any such offer because "he would not permit the Supreme Court of the United States to be brought into politics."[54]

By 1915, however, Woodrow Wilson was president and Republicans thirsted for the White House. With a dearth of attractive candidates and the threat of a Theodore Roosevelt candidacy in the background, Hughes seemed more alluring than ever as the months passed.[55] "No serious discussion of the political outlook fails to include a reference to the possibility that Justice Charles Evans Hughes may be induced to retire from the supreme bench to accept the republican presidential nomination next year," said an Iowa newspaper in March 1915.[56] Hughes did not want to leave the Court, but he thought he would have to accept the Republican nomination if the national convention offered the prize to him. He decided on a course of disavowing interest in the nomination, hoping that an alternative candidate would emerge, and sticking to his judicial work. The problem with that strategy was that, should he become the Republican nominee, he would have to run for president with a minimum of knowledge about the issues of the day with his campaigning days eight years in the past. He did not like Woodrow Wilson, whom he believed had been a snide critic of his governorship, but he over-estimated his own potential effectiveness as a candidate against the president in a national campaign. He hoped that it would not come to that. The only sure way for Hughes to escape the dilemma was an unequivocal statement of withdrawal. Since he did not do that during the first half of 1916, there were Republicans who began to organize an informal, unauthorized Hughes campaign in early 1916. In the process, Hughes became the attractive, electable alternative to a growing prospect that some Republicans found alluring and many others deemed very dismaying, Theodore Roosevelt as a presidential candidate for the Grand Old Party in 1916.

4 THE STATE OF THE DEMOCRATS

In the aftermath of the difficult 1914 elections, Democrats knew that they faced a tough battle to reelect President Wilson. The Republican Party, behind its familiar themes of tariff protection and national defense, seemed confident of victory over their old foe. Observers contended that if the presidential contest had been held in 1914 the Grand Old Party would have secured about 275 electoral votes, 9 more than the 266 needed for success. If accurate, Woodrow Wilson was on his way to becoming a one-term president.[1]

The Democrats understood their underlying predicament. Secretary of the Interior Franklin K. Lane concluded that "the Administration is weak, east of the Alleghanies [*sic*]; and strong west of the Alleghanies." As for Wilson, "the president is growing daily in the admiration of the people. He has little of the quality that develops affection, but this, I think, comes from his long life of isolation."[2] The Democrats would have a difficult sell to make Wilson an attractive candidate.

Having faced the 1914 elections with the economy under stress, the Democrats fretted about what would happen over the next two years. They were very aware of their fate in the 1890s when the economy had collapsed with their party in power. "I have no fear of the outcome of the contest next year, provided we have a restoration of normal times in a business way in this country," wrote Postmaster General Albert Burleson in March 1915. "The European War, if it continues," Burleson believed, "I fear will have such a serious effect on the commercial interests of our country that business depression will become so aggravated that the result in 1916 will be quite uncertain."[3]

Burleson was too pessimistic. A flood of Allied war orders spurred greater prosperity in the spring of 1915 and the administration was more than ready to take full credit for the nation's returning economic health. The Democratic National Committee collected clippings showing the "wonderful prosperity that has come to this nation under this Democratic administration." These "prosperity clippings" were an answer to the previous Republican talk of economic doom.[4]

The Republicans disputed the Democratic invocation of prosperity because "outside of the manufactures of munitions there is very little work in the country and that in many sections while the cost of living is on the increase, men are unable to find jobs." Samuel Gompers, president of the American Federation of Labor, countered "that almost every industry in the country was affected by the stimulus of war orders and men were finding work everywhere."[5]

The most the Republicans could do was label good times as illusory and likely to disappear once the fighting ceased. A favorite phrase among Republicans became that the nation was living in a "fool's paradise" and it would be necessary to return to high tariffs after European nations, no longer at war, began trading with the United States once again. Leaving aside the wisdom of calling those who gained from prosperity deluded, the Republicans were in effect saying that things were fine enough in the present, just the argument the Democrats were advancing. Running against Democratic prosperity was a new experience for Republicans and they struggled to find a real answer to the good times arising from the European conflict.

The Democrats confronted none of the uncertainty about their presidential candidate that the Republicans faced. President Wilson was going to seek another term and would not encounter any dissent from within the party. There was occasional talk that William Jennings Bryan might oppose Wilson on foreign policy grounds, but there was really nothing to such rumors. Occasional attempts to make House Speaker Champ Clark an alternative to Wilson never amounted to anything in the face of strong denials of his candidacy from Clark himself. The exact state of the president's actual popularity among Democrats is hard to measure. Many members of the House and Senate chafed under his leadership, but, like Democrats nationally, they knew that repudiating Wilson would be political suicide.

The major newspapers devoted many pages in their news and editorial columns to looking for signs of impending divisions among the Democrats that, based on historical experience, seemed likely to emerge. The appearance of such splits would make Wilson's reelection impossible. Throughout 1915 Wilson kept the party together in the face of its inherent tendency to separate into its component parts.

The most notable such event occurred during the late spring when Secretary of State William Jennings Bryan resigned over his differences with Wilson regarding the diplomatic response to Germany about the torpedoing of the British liner *Lusitania* on May 7, 1915. Denunciations of Bryan from Republicans were predictable. "Bryan, as usual is an ass," wrote William Howard Taft, "but he is an ass with a good deal of opportunity for mischief."[6] Democrats, surveyed around the country, played down the chances of a lasting split between the president and his former colleague. As one of them put it, "he has resigned from the Cabinet and not from the Democratic party."[7]

Two volatile issues strained the Democratic coalition. Momentum was gathering in the country for the prohibition of the sale of alcoholic beverages. States were going dry as organizations such as the Anti-Saloon League sought to eliminate the liquor power from the nation. Within the Democratic Party, liquor control was strongest in the South and West where rural culture and evangelical religion held sway. Broad sections of the party were increasingly committed to the dry cause. With the president ambivalent and strong for the local option, the issue was not yet one that would rupture the party or deny Wilson's renomination.

Woman suffrage posed more immediate dilemmas for Wilson and his party. The National American Woman Suffrage Association (NAWSA) had been winning state-by-state victories as the preferred road to securing the ballot. At the same time NAWSA had to compete with the more radical campaign for a national constitutional amendment being pursued by Alice Paul and the National Woman's Party. Neither organization really trusted the good motives of the president or his party. Southern Democrats feared that granting the vote to women would lead to calls for blacks to get the ballot.

Wilson himself had private reservations about the wisdom of woman suffrage and he pursued a number of evasive options to avoid a commitment to a constitutional amendment making woman suffrage legal everywhere. As the pressure mounted, he came out for suffrage in the states and declared he would support suffrage in New Jersey in November 1915. The adverse reaction to his second marriage was viewed as one reason for the step. He had married a Washington widow, Edith Bolling Galt, just over a year after the death of his first wife in a union that some of his enemies regarded as unseemly.[8] Suffrage in the states was as far as Wilson was prepared to go as 1915 ended.

Throughout 1915 the press looked for clues of when Wilson would announce for a second term. The Indianapolis speech in January 1915 was seen, according to the newspapers, as one such signal.[9] By May, noting that the Democrats were polling party members about 1916, the headline was "Wilson Seems Choice."[10] Then by August reports said that Wilson was calling party leaders together to plan for the election.[11] And again in early November a New York speech became another moment when presidential intentions would become clear. Wilson again did not supply a hint of his future plans in a speech that focused on preparedness.[12]

Wilson navigated throughout most of 1915 without a serious party division but as the year wound down the issue of preparedness seemed destined to produce what newspapers had long forecast. Although he had dismissed calls for greater spending on defense in December 1914, Wilson could see that the subject was heating up during the following summer. Theodore Roosevelt in particular adopted the cause and spoke out against the alleged weakness of the administration on defense. Believing that the nation's military arm did need bolstering, the president requested from his cabinet officers plans to increase the size of the army and navy.

Wilson's request, which he justified in a speech to the Manhattan Club in New York on November 4, 1915, set off a sustained congressional battle over preparedness. Peace advocates found the proposals of the president dismaying, and agitated their members against the administration. In the process of defending what he had offered, Wilson also attacked elements in society who were disloyal to the United States. He was referring to examples of internal subversion from both within the German government and its spies and elements among German Americans. Wilson's words raised the emotional temperature of politics going into 1916. As Congress reconvened in December, with the election now less than a year away, Wilson stressed preparedness in his annual message. As the British ambassador observed, "The President's own attitude on the subject has completely changed in the last year and he has abandoned the former policy of indifference and skepticism which a short time ago he publicly professed."[13]

The political situation still looked very promising for Republicans. The off-year elections saw woman suffrage in New Jersey go down to defeat, despite Wilson's public support. In the case of New York, the new constitution, which Elihu Root had promoted, also lost. Democrats contended that Progressives were turning Democratic in key states while William Howard Taft proclaimed "the trend is back toward Republicanism."[14] Nothing had happened to shake the GOP faith that victory would be theirs if they found the right candidate.

The Democrats really had no place to go but to the left of the political spectrum in the winter of 1916. Wilson's courtship of the business community had not swayed most of his intended targets from their customary Republican loyalty. There was no realistic prospect of outbidding the GOP with a conservative approach. Doing so, in fact, might alienate the Democratic base without any corresponding gains among Progressives.

As the battle over preparedness went on, Wilson launched a process of reaching out to former Progressives and advocates of social justice. When a vacancy came open on the Supreme Court in late January 1916, Wilson, on his own initiative, named Louis D. Brandeis, known as "the People's Lawyer for his advocacy of progressive causes in the courts," and long identified with reform campaigns. The nomination of Brandeis, a prominent Jew, outraged conservatives such as Taft. Some of the nominee's critics acted from anti-Semitic motives. Their fulminations against his selection added to the popular perception that Wilson had done a progressive thing. When a fight developed in the Senate over Brandeis and his confirmation, the day-by-day struggle underlined the nature of Wilson's move. A letter from Wilson supporting Brandeis at a key point in the struggle demonstrated how committed the president was to his nominee and swept away all doubts about the president's intentions. In his letter to a senator, Wilson contended that his nominee "is a friend of all just men and a lover of the right; and he knows more than how to talk about the right—he knows how to set it forward in the face of its enemies."[15] That Brandeis was Jewish and some of his opponents anti-Semitic made Wilson seem tolerant and inclusive. Reformers were pleased when the Senate finally approved the jurist.

A second area where Wilson moved to confound the Republicans was in an area of their perceived strength, the tariff. As a critic of Republican protective policy, Wilson had long opposed the idea of a tariff commission to investigate rates and recommend changes to Congress. He regarded it as a dodge by supporters of tariffs and not likely to produce lower rates. By late 1915, however, a change of position seemed warranted. The prospect of European competitors "dumping" products in the postwar period loomed larger in the minds of business leaders. Wilson signaled that he had changed his stance in a letter to a prominent House Democrat in late January 1916. It took a while for the Tariff Commission measure, with a proposal for its panel of six members that could recommend alterations in tariff rates, to work its way through Congress, and the final legislation did not come until early September. Republicans realized, however, what Wilson had done to undercut the GOP. Senator Warren G. Harding told a friend: "A good many Republicans think his shift on the question of a tariff commission has helped him and that he has stolen some of our campaign thunder."[16]

Another area where Wilson moved away from his earlier suspicion of federal government action came with rural credits. He had threatened a veto of a bill in 1914 because its effort to direct money to farmers represented in his belief class action to one segment of the economy. But by 1916 the idea was popular in the Middle West and Myron Herrick was supporting the proposal on the Republican side. So Wilson at the end of January gave his backing to a farm credit bill and the measure passed Congress in May.

The surge of Democratic activism attracted notice. A party that for many years had indicated in large part only what it was against had now advanced a positive program. The secretary of the interior, Franklin K. Lane, proclaimed to Wilson: "The Republican party was for half a century a constructive party and the Democratic party was the party of negation and complaint. We have taken the play from them. The Democratic party has become the party of construction."[17]

An influential reform journal tracked the alterations in the president's policies throughout the first half of 1916. *The New Republic* and its editor, Herbert Croly, had little but scathing criticism for the Democrats. In its initial issue in 1915, the editors said that the party "has the vitality of a low organism. It can not only subdivide without losing the continuity of its life, but it can temporarily assume almost any form, any color and any structure without ceasing to recognize itself and without any apparent sacrifice of collective identity."[18] But the editors would change their minds as they watched Wilson and the Democrats become more activist during the spring and summer of 1916.

The Democrats would struggle for several decades with the issue of government activism, but the process of moving to the left that Wilson commenced in the spring of 1916 would endure. The president, despite his earlier suspicions of government power, had now seen the virtues of seeking the votes of former progressives, labor unions, Middle Western farmers, and advocates of social justice. The party remained deaf to the needs of African Americans as it moved toward what would become in time the New Deal coalition. Wilson had intensified segregation within the federal government while his party actively pursued racist policies against blacks, including efforts to repeal the Fourteenth and Fifteenth amendments. As Herbert Croly observed, "the Democrats are now traveling by the light of a pale and fluttering candle which Mr. Wilson has hurriedly contrived out of Republican and Progressive materials."[19]

Wilson's move to the left has, of course, attracted a good deal of attention from historians and biographers. A few years earlier the president had been a champion of limited governmental power who saw the federal government as incapable of supporting woman suffrage, labor unions, and legislation to help specific economic or interest groups in society. That was certainly one of the several Woodrow Wilsons who entered public life in 1910. It was one reason that men like Taft and Root believed that Wilson was nothing more than an opportunist who changed course when expediency dictated. As an exasperated Roosevelt wrote to an English friend, "Wilson trims so as to keep the half-hearted and ignorant, and well-meaning short-sighted people, on his side, and goes on playing Germany's game and making believe to be for a sham-preparedness."[20]

There was more to Wilson than that quick conclusion. The president certainly wanted reelection, and why not? If broadening the reach of the national government was what it took to provide victory for the Democrats, then down that road Wilson would go. The goals were worthy ones after all, and scholars have wondered, in the case of woman suffrage, why it took Wilson so long to do the right thing. He should receive more credit for his capacity for growth and evolution on domestic issues. Consistency in politics is a laudable virtue. So, too, is the capacity to change one's mind when the facts shift.

Wilson's personal foibles contributed to the ire of his opponents. He could be very tricky in his use of language when responding to criticism. Republicans were convinced that the president never really engaged their arguments. His habit after 1915 of calling the Republicans back-ward-looking with out-of-date ideas did not sit well with Republicans, who regarded their Democratic adversaries as sectional and reactionary. Wilson, in short seemed shifty and unprincipled. For Republicans, who often deemed him to be illegitimate because of his minority triumph in 1912, the president grated on them and many of them came to despise Wilson and all his works.

As 1916 opened, however, foreign policy seemed a major part of electoral deliberations as it had not been since the second McKinley-Bryan contest in 1900. While Germany pursued its submarine campaign against the British blockade, Americans feared that their nation would be drawn into the conflict. The president's drive for preparedness touched off a bitter congressional battle in early 1916 as peace Democrats fought against the proposal. "It is distressing to see our party's chances of success destroyed and the country's peace menaced by one in whom we had such great hopes," wrote William Jennings Bryan in February.[21]

While the Democrats debated among themselves about preparedness, a major Republican leader framed the foreign policy issue in a way that would set his party's priorities for the fall campaign to come and thereby challenge the Democrats to respond. On February 15, Elihu Root addressed the New York Republican state convention at Carnegie Hall in New York City. He launched a free-swinging attack on Wilson's war policy. It was a belligerent, caustic address that urged the nation to take a firm stand on how Germany had mistreated Belgium. He accused Wilson of being "brave in words and irresolute in action." Therefore, Root concluded, "No man should draw a pistol who dares not shoot." He arraigned Wilson's policy toward Mexico, especially the American landing at Veracruz in 1914, but it was his denunciation of the administration's stance toward the European war that drew the greatest applause from the enthusiastic audience.[22]

Some of Root's friends and supporters at the convention wanted to seek an endorsement of him as a presidential candidate to accompany the remarks and give him a political lift, but pro-Hughes partisans objected and no actions were taken. The speech caused a great political stir, as Root's orations often did. A British diplomat told his superiors that the Republicans were "going to fight the election on foreign policy."[23]

The Democrats thought instead that the aggressive Root had played right into their hands. Presidential secretary Joseph P. Tumulty wrote to Wilson that "it puts the Republican party in the position of advocating war not only against Germany but against Mexico." As Tumulty summed

"Dressing the Part."
Elihu Root made a bellicose speech in February 1916, and a cartoonist depicted him trying on the attributes of Theodore Roosevelt. Courtesy of the Library of Congress.

matters up, "it means that the Republican party stands for war and the Democratic party for peace with honor."[24] Given the strong sentiment for peace within the country, particularly in the Middle West and beyond the Rockies, the invocation of war in Root's speech actually helped the Democratic case for the party.

The speech stemmed from Root's intense moral feelings about German actions against Belgium and his outrage about Wilson's course. In many respects he felt as strongly opposed to the White House position as

Roosevelt did. Seeing a clear duty for his party, Root marshaled his formidable intellect behind a position that many eastern Republicans shared. In so doing, Root handed the administration an issue they had been evolving toward since the outbreak of the war. As Tumulty put it, a firm stance against American entry into the conflict was a vote-winner. The usually astute Root was in effect urging his party to indict Wilson for not taking strong action that would draw the United States into the fighting.

Root's prescription would have been a wise choice had the Republicans not been themselves divided over what course to pursue. Root's strictures against Germany's treatment of Belgium ran up against the feelings of German Americans in the Middle West who were hoping that their ancestral fatherland would prevail over the Allies. There were other party members, more remote from the East Coast, who wanted to avoid any policy that would risk war. From an electoral standpoint, Root was identifying the GOP with entry into the war, a gift to the Democrats.

The Democrats were eager to accept the donation that Root had made. The former governor of New York, Martin H. Glynn, spoke at the Democratic state convention in Syracuse on March 1 in a detailed rebuttal to Root's arguments. He charged that the Republicans had begun to "treacherously attack" the president and his foreign policy and added "their challenge we gladly accept, confident that a fair-minded American public will uphold the honorable, patriotic, and highly American policy which the Democratic party has pursued beset by difficulties and menaced by pitfalls on every side wherein a single misstep would have plunged this country to disaster and war."[25]

Glynn defended the president and went directly at Root. "Mr. Root may beat his drum and blare his trumpet, but President Wilson will go right on winning the plaudits of the American people by appealing to reason, humanity, and common sense and by keeping the United States the uncompromising champion of the neutral world and the undaunted maintainer of the principles which have guided this nation since 1776."[26]

Noting that Senator Henry Cabot Lodge had made a speech that echoed Root's sentiments, Glynn contended that "both Mr. Root and Senator Lodge say they do not plead for war, and yet they plead to passions which cause war, and when you plead for a cause you plead for its effect." Of Root's indictment about Wilson merely shaking his finger toward belligerents, Glynn replied: "President Wilson has only shaken his finger thus far; when he has to shake his fist the world will find it mailed."[27]

Reviewing what Root had said about Wilson, Mexico, and Europe,

Martin H. Glynn.
A former governor of New York, Glynn made an impressive speech for Wilson at the Democratic Convention in 1916 that sounded the theme of "he kept us out of war." Courtesy of the Library of Congress.

Glynn charged that "Mr. Root would make of the President of the United States an incendiary in a world of fire." Instead, Glynn concluded the president "has persevered, strengthened, dignified and uplifted our noblest national traditions and he will continue to do so no matter what the cost or what the penalty."[28] A British observer agreed that the United States "will follow Wilson any length to keep out of war."[29]

Edward M. House. A close personal friend of President Wilson since 1911, the quiet and secretive Texan played a role in the Wilson reelection campaign. Courtesy of the Library of Congress.

Glynn's speech naturally pleased the president, who told Glynn that his retorts to Root were unanswerable. While the former governor did not say in so many words that Wilson had kept the nation out of war, the thought was there for the Democrats to use at their national convention in the summer. The speech also brought Glynn forward as an effective orator for the Democratic national convention that summer who could articulate the party's message along the lines that House and Wilson wanted.[30]

The challenges of the neutrality situation kept coming. Early in 1916 Democratic unity was threatened when the Gore-McLemore resolution to keep Americans off the ships of belligerents came before lawmakers. Wilson had to employ all of his personal prestige with House members in this battle to block congressional action that would have undercut his authority over foreign policy. With that threat contained, he turned his attention to the election that lay ahead for him and his party. In that process he looked for advice from his close friend and confidant, "Colonel" Edward M. House of Texas.

House and Wilson had become intimate friends before the presidential election of 1912 as Wilson pursued the crucial forty votes of the Texas delegation. Beginning in late 1911, the soft-spoken, wily House achieved a strong influence within the administration though he held no formal position. Younger than Wilson by almost two years, House had inherited wealth in cotton that enabled him to devote his time to the complex politics of Texas in the 1890s. Given his nominal military rank by Governor James S. Hogg, House deployed his fortune and energies in promoting the careers of a number of Texas Democrats who became governor of the state. Historical opinions differ on how powerful House really was in Texas, but his reputation, sometimes self-inflated, preceded him. As House wrote in August 1911, "The people seldom take the man best fitted for the job therefore it is necessary to work for the best man who can be nominated and just now Wilson seems to be that man."[31]

A frail constitution and a retiring manner kept House out of public view. House was a self-promoter who believed himself to be a potential world statesman. With Wilson, he built up his own image and thought himself at least as smart, if not smarter, than the president. As he wrote in 1911, "He is not the biggest man I have ever met but he is one of the pleasantest and I would rather play with him than any prospective candidate I have seen."[32] By 1916, their relationship had undergone some fundamental changes. Wilson's second wife, Edith Wilson, was no friend of House, and she began undermining the Colonel and limiting his influence on her husband. Nonetheless, in the area of presidential politics and for the upcoming contest, House was in his element as a de facto campaign manager who could influence the choice of the individuals who would run the Wilson reelection effort.

A first major concern was naming a qualified Democrat to handle the actual operation of the Wilson campaign. The incumbent chair of the Democratic National Committee was William F. McCombs, a New York lawyer who had held the place since 1912. He and the president were no longer friendly, and Wilson was not about to leave his electoral destiny to the irascible and unreliable McCombs, whose ability to work well with others was dubious.

Working through Colonel House and the financier Bernard Baruch, Wilson secured the resignation of McCombs, and a public exchange of

Vance McCormick. McCormick proved to be an excellent campaign manager for the Wilson effort. Courtesy of the Library of Congress.

letters freed the Wilson men to look elsewhere for a campaign manager. After considering many names, House and the president settled on Vance McCormick of Pennsylvania, the losing gubernatorial candidate in Pennsylvania in 1914. A former mayor of Harrisburg, Pennsylvania, McCormick had played football at Yale where he gained a reputation for toughness. The focused and clever McCormick proved an inspired selection whose skillful direction of the Wilson effort attested to his efficiency.[33]

McCormick in turn assembled an unusually efficient campaign staff to oppose their muscle-bound Republican counterparts. The Wilson organization included Daniel C. Roper, a former member of the Post Office Department, who oversaw the day-to-day workings of the Democratic effort, and Robert Woolley, the director of the Mint, who conducted the publicity bureau for the Democratic National Committee.[34] There were more than a dozen separate departments or bureaus that addressed labor, foreign-born voters, women, and other groups. As Colonel House told the president in late July 1916, "I feel satisfied that we will have the only efficient organization that has ever been constructed in a democratic national campaign."[35] Remembering previous inept Democratic presidential campaigns, the Republicans were not prepared for the efficient team that McCormick had recruited.

A western bureau, under the guidance of Senator Thomas J. Walsh of Montana, in Chicago handled the sending out of the innumerable campaign documents that poured out of the New York headquarters. Walsh told McCormick in early August that "we are starting off under very encouraging conditions." After reviewing the arrangements for the headquarters building, he concluded that it "will not compare in point of eligibility, luxuriousness or extent with those of the Republicans, but I do not imagine that it will suffer any disadvantage on that account."[36]

In planning for the Democratic convention that would assemble in mid-June after the Republicans had made their choice, House spent a good deal of time selecting appropriate speakers. St. Louis had been chosen to shore up Democratic chances in Missouri, which had become a doubtful state after the Republicans carried it in 1904. The state's large German American population also made St. Louis an attractive venue to woo back this disaffected group.[37] That the president would be renominated was a given. The renomination of Thomas Riley Marshall of Indiana as vice president was also taken for granted.

The key point for the Democrats in 1916 was the central position of Indiana in their electoral calculations. They knew that Wilson would have difficulty carrying Middle Western industrial states against the traditional Republican appeal to the protective tariff. Yet, with the vice president from Indiana on the ticket and the Senate majority leader, John Worth Kern, running for a second term, the Democrats wanted to add the bloc of Indiana's votes to the reliably Democratic states in the South where Wilson was unchallenged. The Republicans, too, understood what the state meant in electoral terms. As one of them wrote in May 1916, "we have some of the most proficient political pirates that ever scuttled a ship or cut a throat, and they will sacrifice anybody or anything when it interferes with their personal or financial ends." Both sides prepared to throw money and speakers into the state.[38]

For the convention's keynote speaker, House and Wilson turned again to Martin Glynn, who would read the address the White House had prepared for him and who had the talent to rouse the convention delegates, as his response to Root's speech in February had demonstrated. Glynn would also help with the long-shot Democratic goal of carrying New York against Hughes. Senator Ollie James from Kentucky, another accomplished orator, would follow Glynn as permanent chair of the convention. Both speakers could be relied upon to strike the peace note in their remarks.

By mid-June, Wilson's foreign policy situation seemed to have stabilized in favor of the Democrats and their impending peace-centered campaign. In response to Pancho Villa's attack on Columbus, New Mexico, on March 9, 1916, Wilson had sent a punitive expedition, commanded by General John J. Pershing, into Mexico to pursue and capture the elusive Villa. Faced with the threat of war between the two countries, Wilson resisted pressures for more sustained action and limited American involvement in a manner that most Americans, especially in the West, approved.

So, too, with Germany and its submarines. The French steamer *Sussex* had been torpedoed in the English Channel with some loss of life. In the middle of a crisis like the one that had surrounded the *Lusitania*, Wilson told Berlin that a break in diplomatic relations was imminent. The Germans, not yet prepared to wage unrestricted submarine warfare, said they would not sanction further such attacks. Wilson had prevailed and the so-called Sussex Pledge won popular plaudits. The Democrats had their peace argument for the campaign.

Aware of the likelihood that the Republicans would depict themselves as the custodians of American values in ways that their opponents were not, the president upped the ante by emphasizing how patriotic the Democrats were. Playing the national anthem at frequent intervals was one such touch so that no one could be in any doubt that the president's party was patriotic. The St. Louis convention hall in the crucial border state of Missouri was suffused with an atmosphere of national symbols. Used to the ritual invocation of patriotism when the Republicans gathered, the Democrats sought to go their enemies one better.

The final task for the White House in advance of the convention was to craft the platform that the delegates would adopt. Wilson himself drafted a version of the document that House, Tumulty, and William G. McAdoo then edited, along with suggestions from other interested Democrats. The document praised the record of the administration over the years since 1913, citing the change in tariff policy and the enactment of the Federal Reserve Law. "We indorse the administration of Woodrow Wilson. It speaks for itself. It is the best exposition of sound Democratic policy at home and abroad."[39]

The Democrats struck out at what the platform called groups that sought "the advancement of the interest of a foreign power," and they condemned "all alliances and combinations of individuals" who sought to embarrass or weaken the government "in dealing or negotiating with a foreign power." This plank was included at the express direction of the president. The platform did not specify what groups might be doing such things, but the German-American Alliance was one such target. The Wilson administration thus set in motion some of the response to ethnic tensions that would appear once the United States entered World War I.[40]

While holding on to the Democratic base, Wilson sought to reach out to disaffected Progressives, who were disillusioned with Roosevelt's abandonment of his third party and passionate about social reform. The platform endorsed an array of progressive proposals including national child labor legislation, rural credits, government support for highway construction, and the eight-hour day. Only on woman suffrage did the platform adhere to Wilson's preference for state action over a national amendment. The document offered no specific praise of the power of government to enact and implement such goals. That would have raised worries among southerners and party conservatives about the reach of such power. On woman suffrage, the delegates stuck to Wilson's position in favor of state action, and thus gave the Republicans an opening on the issue if they chose to take it.

The national convention coalesced around the themes of peace, prosperity, and progressivism toward which the administration had been moving since 1914. Observers reported that "The Convention at St. Louis was a revival meeting, swayed by genuine human feeling."[41] The crowd rocked when Martin Glynn and Ollie James in their speeches described how Wilson's policies had prevented the nation from entering the European War. Citing historical instances when the presidents had refrained from aggressive action, Glynn repeated, at the behest of the delegates, "We did not go to war" to an enthusiastic response from the audience. As one newspaper recorded, "Glynn gave convention the oratory it wanted."[42]

The next day, Ollie James lavished praise on Wilson because "without orphaning a single American child, without widowing a single American mother, without firing a single gun, without the shedding of a single drop of blood, he [Wilson] wrung from the most militant spirit that ever brooded above a battlefield an acknowledgment of American rights and an agreement to American demands." The transported delegates, awash with fervor, begged James to repeat his words with abundant cheers. As a Republican reporter told Taft, "'Peace' was the great card played up by Glynn and James at St. Louis, and it was the only one that stirred applause and enthusiasm."[43] The Democratic platform writers added the phrase "he kept us out of war" to the document to underline the point. The Democrats were in an unfamiliar position. Their convention had revealed no serious party splits, no dissent about the president, and a confident spirit going into the campaign. "Like the assembling of a clan on the eve of battle, the Convention therefore turned itself into a ceremonial meeting for the Presidential contest yet to come."[44]

The immediate verdict on the St. Louis convention among commentators was that the Democrats had established their major themes going into the fall campaign. As George Harvey wrote in the *North American Review*, "a convention, personally conducted from Washington, which opened listlessly, became thoroughly enlivened and the great body of delegates who first entered the hall disspirited and dejected finally left full of enthusiasm and, if not of confidence, at least as firm a determination to hold the offices as that of the Republicans to get them."[45] The New York *World*, the nation's leading Democratic paper, argued that "By consistent, unswerving adherence to a policy of peace and neutrality, President Wilson has kept the United States in a position where militarism has been humbled and the lawless thrustings of belligerency stopped by the sheer compelling force of American ideals."[46]

There was no modern polling to determine whether Wilson got a "bounce" out of the convention, but it seems likely that the press reports solidified the impression of a party united to avoid any hint of future overseas participation in the war. For the Republicans, who had already nominated Hughes as their choice, the cohesion of the Democrats in the convention and the emergence of the peace theme came as an unsettling shock. Perhaps the long-anticipated GOP triumph was not to be so certain after all. It would be more important than ever that Hughes live up to his advance billing as a credible, persuasive challenger to the president. The manner in which Hughes had been chosen, the role of Theodore Roosevelt, and the ultimate destination of disaffected Progressives, all these were elements in the mix as the 1916 campaign got under way in that presidential election summer.

5 THE SELECTION OF HUGHES AND THE LAUNCHING OF THE REPUBLICAN CAMPAIGN

The specter haunting the Republicans during the first half of 1916 was the possibility that Theodore Roosevelt might secure the Republican presidential nomination on what was regarded as a pro-war platform. Elihu Root well stated the fears of loyal Republicans in mid-May 1916. If Roosevelt and the Progressives, he told Henry L. Stimson, "sought to insist upon the rule or ruin policy with T.R. and to black-jack us into accepting him as dictator when the sentiment of the Republican convention was clearly against it, it would be the end of any future party loyalty."[1]

To understand the dilemma that Roosevelt's candidacy in 1916 posed for regular Republicans like Root and Stimson requires some discussion of how members of the GOP saw themselves in those days. In their mind, the Republicans were the only political organization in the nation that embodied true American values. They had saved the Union during the Civil War and advanced basic American principles by their very existence in the years that followed. To restore the rightful balance of American politics, it was imperative that Wilson be defeated.[2] The problem with Roosevelt, beyond his betrayal in 1912, was that he was likely to lose four years later. His calls for preparedness were seen as signs of Roosevelt's eagerness to enter the fighting at an early date. In the Middle Western states, where peace sentiment was strong, a Roosevelt candidacy would give key states to the president, or so Republican politicians believed. It made sense in their minds to find a candidate other than Roosevelt who could tap anti-Wilson sentiments without calling into play the former president's liabilities, or threatening entry into the war.[3]

By the spring of 1916, the race for the Republican nomination had narrowed down to two men, Roosevelt and Hughes. Elihu Root had some residual strength, particularly in New York, but he was not seen as a serious challenger to the front-runners. The various contenders from their home states—John Weeks, Charles Fairbanks, and Lawrence Sherman—had not shown real national appeal. "It is Hughes against the field," wrote Gus Karger in early June, "and unless the situation should change materially, he will be nominated."[4]

In the case of Roosevelt, his motives had emerged with clarity in the late winter. While he and his wife were on a trip to the French West Indies, he gave out a statement on March 9 that asserted that "it would be a mistake to nominate me unless the country has in its mood something of the heroic—unless it feels not only devotion to ideals but the purpose measured to realize those ideals in action." Advocating universal military service, denouncing the German-American Alliance for disloyalty, he made it clear that he would run on a platform that would place the United States on the side of the Allies at an early date.[5]

In a speech in Kansas City on Memorial Day, Roosevelt spoke of how the warring nations were sending men to distant parts of the globe and warned Americans of the possible consequences of an invasion. At the same time, he was making the implicit point that an American army, raised through universal service, could be sent to Europe. Roosevelt was thus invoking the prospect of war while attacking German Americans, the key voting bloc in the Middle West. Huge crowds, including some German Americans drawn by Roosevelt's charisma, cheered what Roosevelt said in Detroit and Kansas City, but professional politicians saw crucial states slipping to Wilson if Roosevelt were selected.[6]

There was much noise and ballyhoo in the enthusiasm for Roosevelt, but he did not win the delegates he needed in states such as Massachusetts and Michigan. As the Republican convention opened on June 7 in Chicago, it was clear that Roosevelt was not going to win the GOP prize.[7] Unlike 1912, when Roosevelt attended the convention, this time he remained in Oyster Bay at the end of a telephone line connected to George W. Perkins in Chicago and a stenographer taking notes.[8] From this telephonic vantage point, he was prepared to wheel and deal to get the most out of his situation.

Roosevelt could still count on the support of what lingered of the Progressive Party, which was to meet in Chicago at the same time as the Republicans. If Roosevelt ran again on a third-party ticket, he would lose and likely insure a Wilson victory. So he hoped to use the existence of the Progressives to induce the Republicans to endorse his position or perhaps nominate him after all. A committee of Progressives and Republicans sought to find some common ground on the platform and a nominee. The platform proved easy enough to accomplish but the Republicans simply would not hear of Roosevelt. The convention delegates in the GOP meeting were convinced that Hughes was a winning candidate while Roosevelt would lose. Roosevelt thought of Hughes as "a man of the Wilson type" but the only alternative he could offer to the Progressives was Henry Cabot Lodge.[9] It was a fatuous choice that outraged the members of the third party. They felt betrayed and they nominated Roosevelt anyway. Roosevelt declined their nomination and two weeks later endorsed Hughes as everyone expected. The Progressive Party was dead as both Hughes and Wilson sought the votes of what remained. A bitter William Allen White later recalled that it was "the ebb tide for our cause. We looked out across the dark stretches of the dirty marsh where once our current flowed so strong, and in the agony of disillusion and despair we saw the dark rocks and the crawling things that had been underneath that ebbing tide."[10]

In all the furor over Roosevelt and the Progressives in June 1916, the forces that led to the nomination of Hughes have been denigrated as professional politicians out to name what seemed to be the most electable candidate. That is an odd argument. What party does not seek a candidate most pleasing to the electorate? Hughes emerged in the first half of 1916 as the probable nominee because Republicans believed he would give them the best chance to win in November. He could, they presumed, carry his home state of New York, run well in the Middle West, and carry the traditionally Republican bastions in the West.[11] He would make a campaign on the protective tariff, rouse the electorate, and oust the hated Wilson.

The sentiment for Hughes had gathered momentum early in the year. As a reporter for the New York *Herald* wrote in early April, Hughes was "strong because of the atmosphere of uncertainty or mystery with which he has surrounded himself."[12] Republicans of all stripes and ideas could imagine Hughes as a forceful anti-Wilson spokesman for their point of view. Remembering the Youngstown speech, they expected Hughes to do to the president what the New York governor had done to Bryan. His unofficial campaign, which he neither endorsed nor encouraged, had as its manager Frank H. Hitchcock. The former postmaster general in the Taft cabinet, Hitchcock had directed the Taft presidential campaign in 1908 to a thumping victory over Bryan. His expertise reassured the professionals that Hughes was a potential winner over Wilson.[13] However, Hitchcock had made enemies in 1908 and as Taft's postmaster general and these adversaries worried about Hitchcock as the potential manager of a Hughes campaign.

As for the Justice himself, he did not want to be nominated, as his public comments made clear, but he did not see how he could turn down the nomination if it came to him as a unanimous action of the Republican delegates. Unfortunately, that posture put Hughes in the worst possible position to be an eventual candidate. He could not prepare himself for what would happen if he were nominated, and did not sort out where he stood on most of the pressing issues of the day. Obviously at some personal level Hughes wanted to be president and believed that he could be a successful candidate just on the basis of his innate ability. To some degree, Hughes overrated his own talents and failed to recognize what a formidable foe the president would be in an actual race.

If Hughes felt a certain sense that he was destined to be president, his feeling might well have stemmed from the letters he was receiving imploring him to run. One such missive came in April from William Howard Taft who, after reviewing the announced or potential Republican candidates told Hughes, "You will certainly be elected if you accept this nomination and you will reunite the only party from which constructive progress can be expected at a most critical time in the country's history." Hughes, like most Republicans, shared Taft's view that the Democrats represented "the organized incapacity of the country" and he disliked Wilson's foreign policy and record on the tariff. The prospect of a virtual coronation at the hands of the party to which he had belonged all his life must have gone into the mental calculations that engaged Hughes as the nomination became more and more probable.[14]

Because of the contempt that Republicans felt for Democrats in general and Wilson in particular, they believed that the upcoming presidential race would not be particularly difficult. Some observers, such as Taft, recognized that Wilson's ability to keep the nation out of the war made him popular, but they still expected that the nomination of Hughes and the familiar themes of tariff protection and national defense would carry the day. The Republicans were so accustomed to winning national elections that the prospect that Wilson might win was virtually inconceivable.

With the popular tide in the party running toward Hughes, the Republicans assembled in Chicago and opened proceedings at the national convention on June 7. The weather was stormy and rainy and unseasonably cold for early June. The delegates knew that Hughes was likely to win the nomination. Their enthusiasm for his selection was tepid, but they expected him to defeat the hated Wilson. The keynote speaker was Warren G. Harding, elected to the Senate from Ohio two years earlier. He informed the delegates that "the allied hosts of the believers in Republican principles are in a vast majority in the country—when the banners of harmony are unfurled." He added that "no party can endure which is not progressive," which came down to a better national defense, higher tariffs, maintenance of neutrality, and making "social justice and attending welfare typical of our national life." Nowhere did Harding endorse specific domestic policies other than a reiteration of the tariff. According to Colonel House, Harding's remarks were "tame," notable more for platitudes than for precise criticisms of the Wilson administration, while a prominent Democrat reported a consensus that the speech was "a frost."[15]

The nomination process opened on June 9 with the speeches on behalf of the various candidates. Governor Charles S. Whitman of New York did the honors for Hughes, who was still adhering to the position of silence he had maintained throughout the year. Whitman proclaimed that "we are here in response to the demand of the American people that a minority president give way to a leader representing the will of the majority." To that end he nominated Hughes, a man "sterling in his Republicanism, and free from the animosities engendered by factional strife, his private life above suspicion, his public life without a flaw, a great lawyer, an effective campaigner, and an able executive, a mature statesman, a learned jurist, he above all others combines the essential qualifications of a true leader in the crisis of the party and of the nation." The reference to Hughes's private life was an allusion to recurrent Republican whispers about Wilson's alleged infidelity to his first wife, while the assertion that Hughes was a good campaigner looked back to the Youngstown address.[16]

The first ballot revealed the underlying disposition of the delegates. Hughes led the field with 253½ votes, half the number needed for the

Charles W. Fairbanks. To run with Hughes and to help the Republicans carry Indiana, the party selected Fairbanks, who had been vice president under Theodore Roosevelt between 1905 and 1909. It was not an inspiring choice. Courtesy of the Library of Congress.

nomination. Roosevelt trailed the numerous favorite sons with only 81 votes. A second ballot raised the total for Hughes to 326. Roosevelt tailed off to 65 votes. It was evident as the delegates adjourned for the night that Hughes was likely to be chosen the next day unless something unusual took place. In the cloistered atmosphere of the Supreme Court, Hughes still hoped he would not be nominated, but events were now beyond his control.

By the morning of June 10, it was all over. On the third ballot Hughes achieved a total of 949½ votes. Roosevelt slumped to just 19 delegates in his favor. The Hughes nomination was made unanimous, and the Republicans awaited word of what Hughes would do as the Republican nominee. As his potential running mate the convention chose Charles W. Fairbanks of Indiana, who had been Roosevelt's vice president from 1905 to 1909. Fairbanks might help the party in Indiana, but otherwise he added little to the ticket. Fairbanks tried to withdraw but was nominated before his wire arrived. Since the convention had adjourned, "under the circumstances I felt it my duty to accept."[17]

Hughes now faced the decision he had avoided throughout 1916. At the urging of other justices and with the conviction that Wilson should be replaced, Hughes concluded that he now had to run for president and he believed he would be elected.[18] He wrote a terse letter of resignation from the Court to Wilson and prepared a telegram to the assembled Republicans accepting their nomination. Hughes wired his acceptance on June 10. "I have not desired the nomination. I have wished to remain on the bench." But with the call of the convention for a protective tariff and preparedness, "I cannot fail to answer with the pledge of all that is in me to the service of our country." He indicted Wilson's policy toward Mexico, condemned the erosion of the diplomatic corps in such cases as that involving Myron Herrick, and advocated greater preparedness. On domestic issues, the tariff came first. "In preventing, as we must, unjust discrimination and monopolistic practices, we must still be zealous to assure the foundations of honest business." He promised an efficient and impartial administration. Nowhere did he mention Wilson by name or criticize the Democratic Party. It was a sign of the campaign to come.[19] The delegates felt more optimism about their nominee. "Something of that buoyant spirit born of the prospect of victory, so noticeably lacking in the convention itself, began to manifest itself."[20]

"The results of the Convention have been splendid," wrote George Wickersham, Taft's former attorney general. "Hughes is in fine fighting trim and his telegram of acceptance has already put the Democrats on the defensive."[21] In the initial flurry of enthusiasm over at last having Hughes nominated, Republican hopes expanded. As the president of Columbia University, Nicholas Murray Butler, told James Bryce in England, "The nomination of Mr. Hughes has been received with the utmost enthusiasm by the Independent voters and by a large fraction of the Progressives. The Progressive party as such is dead as a door nail. Three-fourths of their number, including all the more rational and sane, will support Mr. Hughes."[22]

Eight days after the selection, the *New York Times* visited the hastily assembled Hughes headquarters in a New York hotel. "It is the most cheerfully cocksure and confident headquarters from which a campaign was ever directed. The casual visitor could think it was all over except the inauguration."[23] People in the Hughes campaign were already allocating future diplomatic posts to insiders within the Hughes organization. The old-time Hughes alliance of his governorship was revived and it intended to work independent of the national committee. "Its campaign specialty will be to urge the voters throughout the country that this is a year for non-partisanship in so far as non-partisanship consists of a

Democrat voting for a Republican."[24] They did not regard that task as especially difficult.

Hughes commenced writing his acceptance speech in June, consulting with party leaders, and thinking about the post of chair of the Republican National Committee, who would provide the daily direction while Hughes made speeches. He was also concerned to secure the support of Theodore Roosevelt, which came on June 22, and the Progressive National Committee voted 32 to 6 to endorse Hughes on June 26. The candidate began laying plans for an August speaking tour that would take him to the West Coast.

The most immediate decision that Hughes had to make was the selection of his campaign manager. Frank Hitchcock ruled himself out because of his central part in the Hughes nomination. In any event there was significant opposition within the party to Hitchcock and to other stalwarts such as Taft's secretary Charles D. Hilles who had run the losing campaign in 1912.[25] As the days proceeded, Hughes turned increasingly to an old and trusted political friend, William R. Willcox, president of the New York City Board of Education. Long active in New York City politics, Willcox had been postmaster in the city in the second Roosevelt administration and on the Public Service Commission under Hughes. One of his many advocates contended that Willcox "has three advantages. He is a personal friend of Mr. Hughes, he has the ability, and he is in a position to unite all branches of the party." Willcox enjoyed the backing of Mrs. Hughes and Governor Whitman as well.[26]

The defeat of Charles Evans Hughes in 1916 would cast his wife back into the historical shadows, but her role in his campaign was a significant one. Although she told the press that "I cannot bear, and never will be able to, to see myself quoted in print,"[27] she campaigned by her husband's side all over the country wearing a miner's lamp and other regalia on occasion. She insisted that he not strain his voice by speaking out-of-doors and that he not make appearances on Sundays. She was reported to favor woman suffrage and was regarded as "of the type of woman who is always busy."[28] When it looked for a day in November that Hughes had won, the Washington *Evening Star* said that, as the presumptive first lady, "she has acquired a wide acquaintance in its resident and official circles and a thorough knowledge of the intricacies of its etiquette."[29] When Charles Evans Hughes at last gets a modern biography, Antoinette Hughes should get her due.

In the post-convention euphoria of the Hughes selection, little imme-

Hughes and Willcox.
The selection of William R. Willcox to run the Hughes campaign proved to be one of the large mistakes of 1916. Willcox was photographed with the presidential candidate, Mrs. Hughes (right), and another woman. Courtesy of the Library of Congress.

diate attention was given to the qualifications of the proposed campaign manager. The thick-set, mustachioed Willcox was fifty-four, with no experience in national politics and scant progressive bona fides. How close he was to Hughes was not clear. After the election, Hughes played down his proximity to Willcox and said only in his autobiographical notes that "without disparaging the zeal, integrity, and personal devotion of William R. Willcox, I think that if Will Hays had been the manager of my presidential campaign it would have been successful," leaving the impression that someone other than Hughes himself had selected Willcox.[30]

When the selection was announced, Colonel House told Wilson: "I am glad Hughes has chosen Willcox to manage his campaign. He is not an able man and is anything but progressive."[31] Wilson concurred: "It means nothing or, rather, if it means anything, it means that Hughes is compromising with the influences which I expect ultimately to pull him down."[32]

The selection of Willcox reflected the desire of the candidate to put his personal imprint on the campaign, which he and other Republicans expected to be a rather easy contest along the lines of Taft's victory over Bryan in 1908. In these preliminary calculations, the electoral map tilted toward the GOP. They assumed a basic 250 plus electoral votes in the Hughes column, with his home state furnishing the largest bloc at 45. He began very close to the 266 electoral votes needed to win. Adding to his potential strength in the Northeast were such states as Pennsylvania (38), New Jersey (14), Massachusetts (18), Connecticut (7), Maine (6), Vermont (4) and Rhode Island (3). In this region tariff protection should carry the day. Looking at the Middle West, Republicans counted on bastions such as Illinois (29), Michigan (15), Indiana (15), Ohio (24), Minnesota (12), and Wisconsin (13). By these calculations, Hughes and his party would have more than 200 electoral votes. Based on historical performance, so it was believed, the western states of California (13), Washington (7), Kansas (10), Colorado (6), North Dakota (5), and New Mexico (3) would put Hughes over the top. In their most optimistic moments, Hughes and his aides could envision a result that gave the candidate more than 300 electoral votes and victory.[33]

It's not exactly clear the ways that Willcox fell short as a campaign manager. His main task was to coordinate the efforts of the GOP professionals who had been through so many contests before. He seems to have lacked the capacity to inspire the people around him and to impart focus to the canvass. He aided Hughes in his strategy of conciliating conservatives within the party but he could not convince the candidate to change his speaking style when complaints came that Hughes was not connecting with audiences.

As the country and the party waited with excitement for Hughes to launch his campaign, the candidate confronted the dilemmas that would haunt his effort down to election day. The buzz around his nomination raised expectations that he would repeat his Youngstown performance and sound a clarion call to Americans disillusioned with Wilson's leadership. But what was he going to say? On the issue of neutrality and the European war, he had to please pro-Allied Republicans from the East Coast who wanted a hard line against Germany and submarines while not angering the German Americans and the peace progressives from the Middle West. He could and did attack the president's performance in Mexico, but that raised the question of whether he favored greater American intervention there with the inevitable chance of war.

On domestic issues, Hughes could not take the Republicans to a more advanced position on reform subjects. He did not favor such a stance personally and he would have drawn opposition from within the Republican ranks. There was one issue that seemed a means of distinguishing himself from Wilson in a way that would appeal to reformers—woman suffrage. If he came out for a national constitutional amendment, he would be in a more progressive posture than Wilson, who stuck to his views that states should decide whether or not to let women vote. This stance, it was presumed, would attract pro-suffrage voters in the West angry at Wilson. It would also demonstrate sympathy for progressivism at a low political cost. Anti-suffrage voters might be vexed but they would find other reasons to support Hughes. The leaders of the militant National Woman's party and the more moderate National American Woman Suffrage Association all assured Hughes of the electoral gains that would flow from such a decision.

With women voting in significant numbers for the first time in western states and with Wilson stuck with his state suffrage position, an opening for Hughes to co-opt the suffrage vote presented itself. On August 1, he met with members of the Women's Roosevelt League for Hughes at the Astor Hotel and stated: "I announced last night, I was in favor of the Federal amendment." He told his audience that "there is an incurable defect of character in the Administration with respect to the weakness and vacillation which have characterized it, and we cannot expect improvement from that source." Since he believed that "the granting of a vote to women is inevitable," he now favored the amendment approach.[34]

It must have seemed an easy way to get to the left of Wilson on a sensitive issue and so Hughes acted. As it turned out the move was far from decisive. Gus Karger put it well on July 19 as signs indicated that Hughes would endorse the amendment. "It may give him an advantage with women voters—I am not in a position to gauge it—but it will not give additional joy to a good many others whose disposition even now is merely to vote the ticket for him without undertaking to persuade any of the neighbors to come along."[35]

The candidate had several topics to balance during June and July as he wrote party leaders for advice and to familiarize himself with current issues after six years on the bench. While wooing progressives, he reassured regulars that he was an "organization Republican." By putting ten Republicans and five Progressives on the executive committee, "the bloody chasm is bridged," in the words of a Republican journalist.[36] Aware of his reputation for irritating regular Republicans while governor, Hughes seems to have decided not to do anything that would revive that problem. As would soon appear in California, that was a fateful judgment.

Attention thus focused on the acceptance speech that would reveal the real Hughes to the political world as a national figure. "His speech of acceptance is to outline the issues and leave nothing unsaid that may be said now." Republicans assumed that Hughes would take the offensive against Wilson with an aggressive speech, but Gus Karger wondered if Hughes was "a little hard-up for issues" as he worked on his address.[37] Taft and others believed, however, that there were ample flaws in the Wilson record to sustain a full-throated denunciation of the president and his administration. Republicans looked for a trumpet call that would begin the defeat of Wilson and his party.

As Hughes scanned the political terrain he came to conclusions that dictated a different path to the White House. For example, he decided not to mention Wilson's name in his litany of criticisms. While deferring to the dignity of the presidential office, Hughes at least at the outset did not draw the lines between himself and the incumbent with any passion. Not wishing to paint himself into a corner on hot questions, Hughes decided to emphasize themes of Americanism and efficiency. Inevitably such an approach was somewhat bloodless and detached, blurring the differences and creating doubt about what Hughes would do on the tough issues of peace and war. It is not clear whether Hughes sought comments on his speech in advance; he kept to himself and only Mrs. Hughes and perhaps Willcox were likely to have been in his confidence.

The Republicans did all they could to make the acceptance speech a great occasion at Carnegie Hall on July 31. They could not control the summer heat and there was no air-conditioning. Warren G. Harding introduced the candidate. The attending throng included Theodore Roosevelt and a bevy of senators, party dignitaries, and 3,500 listeners. The *New-York Tribune* called it a "love feast of the reunited Republicans and Progressives who shook hands, cheered and mopped perspiring brows together in token of their rediscovered brotherhood."[38]

It had all the ingredients of a triumphal moment except for the speech and the candidate. Choosing the title "America First and America Efficient," Hughes read his 8,000-word remarks to the sweltering audience. Hughes was ordinarily a somewhat dry and legalistic speaker, not much given to rhetorical flourishes or prepared applause lines. At the outset, he assailed the diplomatic personnel of the Wilson administration as political appointees and their performance as a "dismal record for those who believe in Americanism." He cited the recall of Myron T. Herrick as wartime ambassador to France as a case in point. It was a reasonable criticism, but far from the red meat the crowd was expecting. He followed that allegation with a lengthy critique of Wilson's Mexican policy in which he promised "a new policy, a policy of firmness and consistency through which alone we can promote an enduring friendship." What he meant in practice by "firm, consistent and friendly dealing" with Mexico, he did not say.[39]

When it came to domestic issues, Hughes sought to strike as progressive a note as his conservative party would allow him to go. He termed the wartime prosperity "a fool's paradise" and warned of the dangers to American trade when the fighting ended. Whether it made sense to accept that times were good under the Democrats, he did not ask. Rather he invoked the virtues of the protective tariff, sounding like a stand-pat politician. He asked for a more effective transportation system, promotion of business enterprise, and support for the merchant marine, but not Wilson's 1915 ship purchase proposal.

On questions relating to labor, he was for arbitration of disputes, workmen's compensation, as well as rural credits for agriculture. He favored retention of the Philippines, woman suffrage by a national amendment, and greater efficiency in government. He ended the speech by saying: "We have a vision of America prepared and secure; strong and just; equal to her tasks; an exemplar of the capacity and efficiency of a free people. I endorse the platform adopted by the Convention and accept its nomination."[40]

Hughes gave a good speech by ordinary partisan standards, which drew public praise from his fellow Republicans for its emphasis on the tariff.[41] Democrats were predictably unimpressed. Joe Tumulty called the speech "flat and ineffective."[42] A major line of criticism from the Democrats was that Hughes had offered little indication of what he would do differently than Wilson. "Has Mr. Hughes any issue, any program, or has he nothing but a lawyer's criticism of detail?" asked Norman Hapgood, a party journalist for Wilson.[43] The essential problem for Hughes and his acceptance were the immense expectations that had been aroused. When he proved something less than a spell-binding orator, the disappointment was profound. The young, liberal reporter Walter Lippmann called the event "a dismal affair" and said of Hughes, "I had never realized before how common place his mind is."[44] For the Democrats, they had the abrupt perception that the Republican candidate had not lived up to his advance billing and the president now could win reelection after all. The election would be a real battle and not a Republican walkover.

Already there were discouraging reports out of national Republican headquarters about the quality of Willcox's leadership. "Work at the Astor [hotel] is not progressing as well as at the Democratic headquarters," wrote a Republican. "Mr. Willcox appears to be very nervous and I think he tries to do too much."[45]

Hughes had scheduled a national tour to begin in mid-August. He wanted to introduce himself to the public to counter the impression that he was cold and aloof in his personal manner. That stereotype dogged him throughout the campaign, despite his own and Republican efforts to soften his image. The Republicans made movies of the candidate "in various poses showing him in his home and with his family" to assist the public in seeing "what a genial individual the Republican nominee really is."[46] At a meeting with Republican editors the day after the acceptance speech, he told them "that one of the things he had to live down was his reputation of 'not being human.'" Since it had now arisen once again, "he had determined to live down the reputation once for all."[47]

While Hughes participated in any number of campaign events to showcase his humanity, he did not do anything to change or improve his rather austere oratorical style. Theodore Roosevelt, who knew well about such matters, warned him that what "the average voter wants is not an etching, but a poster, a statement so broad and clear in such simple language that he can thoroughly understand it."[48] If Hughes got the message he did not incorporate into his addresses, which continued to be free of crowd-pleasing touches such as laugh-lines or anecdotes. He was who he was and he was not about to adjust to please his critics.

Before the candidate departed for his campaign swing across the country, he and Willcox decided that Hughes would defer to local Republicans in the various states and stay out of bitter factional battles. In California, that meant letting the old-guard party members who were opposing Governor Hiram Johnson in his race for the U.S. Senate escort Hughes everywhere. Hughes had already sent the fiery governor a telegram thanking him for his support, another small gesture that did not sit well with party conservatives. Johnson had been Roosevelt's running mate in 1912 and had used his executive powers to keep Taft off the Cali-

Hughes, son, and grandson.
To offset the severe and aloof public image of Hughes, the Republicans tried to humanize him with portraits of his family. Courtesy of the Library of Congress.

fornia ballot in 1912 so that Roosevelt could carry the state. Beyond that, the regulars regarded Johnson as an unprincipled demagogue and hated him with a passion otherwise reserved for Wilson.[49]

Hughes began his tour in Detroit where before a large crowd he promised "to see that American rights are safeguarded and that America's name, in administration, in policy, and in execution is honored throughout the world." Republicans told the *New York Times* that "the long hoped-for 'punch' had been put into the Hughes campaign," a tacit admission of what the acceptance speech had lacked. Hughes partisans also asserted that the candidate had answered the "What would you do?" question about Mexico: Hughes himself repeated that question and gave his answer, another indicator that the Democrats had made a point about his failure to present alternatives. Hughes was also heckled at various moments when he was speaking about preparedness and Mexico.

Based on information that reporters from Republican newspapers shared with their readers, Hughes enjoyed good crowds and enthusiastic responses on his national tour. Yet even these laudatory stories acknowledged that the candidate was sticking to his themes of efficiency and preparedness. Moreover, some of his criticisms seemed rather petty. He took pride in denying, for example, White House claims that the director of the census, E. Dana Durand, had left his post voluntarily. Hughes read a letter from Durand saying that had been forced to resign to validate his charge.[50]

He also raised anti-southern charges of sectionalism in Butte, Montana. There were stories that disclosed, when Hughes talked about the tariff, "he has taken note from the indifferent attitudes of the crowds that have faced him west of the Rocky Mountains."[51] Benjamin B. Lindsey, the municipal court judge in Denver, Colorado, told Roosevelt that the mention of his name when Hughes spoke accounted for "the only big enthusiasm at the meetings here," adding that "there was none of the old time rousing enthusiasm. The whole thing was rather flat."[52]

Because in the end California completed Wilson's victory, the trip that Hughes made to that state and his alleged snub of Hiram Johnson at a California hotel have become famous. As Spencer Olin and other historians have noted, the real snub of Johnson lay in the decision of Hughes and his advisers, concerned about party loyalty, to put themselves in the hands of the anti-Johnson forces from the moment the candidate's train reached the California state line.

All arrangements were under the supervision of Johnson's bitterest enemies in the state, William H. Crocker of the Southern Pacific Railroad and Francis V. Keesling, a leader of the conservative Republicans. Governor Johnson was running in the GOP primary for the U.S. Senate and his opponents planned to give him no access to Hughes while the presidential nominee was in the state.

Events included a meal at an anti-union open shop, the Commer-

Hiram Johnson. Because California went for Wilson, much attention was devoted to Hughes and his alleged "snub" of the progressive governor. Johnson undercut the Hughes campaign. Courtesy of the Library of Congress.

cial Club, where the management refused even the small gesture of taking down placards boasting of its commitment to the open shop. Labor could accept the presence of nonunion waiters if the sign was removed. When asked to go along with this token gesture, the reply was: "Take down those placards? Not on your life. We have got these *labor bastards* in this town where we want them and we are not going to let up on them at all."[53] The placards stayed, and labor union supporters linked Hughes with the decision. At a rally in the city, Hughes added that "with local differences I have no concern," a remark that Progressives found demeaning to their cause.[54] There is no evidence that he had any qualms about dining under those circumstances. As a result, union members voted against Hughes and for Wilson in San Francisco.

The crucial moment for Hughes in historical terms came at the Virginia Beach Hotel in Long Beach where Hiram Johnson was also staying on August 20. The governor and the candidate missed connections in what some termed a snub of the governor. Nothing was deliberate. Hughes only learned later that Johnson was present. There was no snub as such about the missed hotel encounter. The key point was that Hughes had aligned himself with the conservatives throughout his days in California, much to the ire of the Johnson partisans and their leader.

"Hughes had better not have come here," wrote a leading progressive figure to Theodore Roosevelt. "He distinctly lost by his visit. Ordinarily the state is predominantly Republican. I would put it today in the doubtful class."[55]

As Hughes rested from his exertions on his trip west, there were signs that his campaign was in trouble. Frank Hitchcock was welcomed back to the enterprise and "given a roving commission to discover the cause of the lack of 'pep' and apply the remedy by election day." Newspapers reported that Chairman Willcox was not pleased with this development but was told "that if a master hand was not laid on the machine it might go to pieces." Reporters noted after the western swing the presence of "strong pacifist sentiment" in the region and the impact of unparalleled prosperity and predicted that the nation was "likely to witness such a close contest as that which elected Cleveland over Blaine in 1884." That prospect was not what Republicans had anticipated when Hughes was boomed in the spring.[56]

Charles Evans Hughes was an outstanding legal mind, as his later service as Chief Justice of the United States demonstrated, but he was a mediocre presidential candidate. After leaving the Court to accept the Republican nomination, he decided that he wanted to be president after all, and threw himself into the fray against Wilson and the Democrats. As he did so, he kept the self-confidence in his own abilities and refusal to emulate the ways of ordinary politicians. He insisted on the theme of efficiency as the hallmark of his campaign even though it lacked excitement and bite for the crowds that turned out to hear him. It was as if he were running to be city manager of the United States instead of president. His emphasis on the tariff as his main domestic priority gave his campaign a slightly musty feel, looking back to the glory days of the Republicans in the 1890s. Audiences came to cheer the Republican nominee and found themselves bored after half an hour of his strictures against Wilson. A Minnesota newspaper editor summed up the problem for the candidate: "He was the Supreme Court judge, and the people were ready for a message. Had that message been given without regard for details at this time, Mr. Hughes would have come home from his trip a strong candidate. Because he did not give the people what they were looking for, he made no headway with the independent voters."[57]

By the end of August, the Democratic leaders, who had feared the nomination of Hughes, were delighted with his faltering performance on the stump and confident about Wilson's chances in November. The

New York Times said on its editorial page that "the Republicans were looking for a volcano. They are getting the most gigantic, prolonged cold shower that ever fell."[58] An Oregonian told William G. McAdoo that the history of the Republicans could be related in two chapters from John C. Fremont the Great Pathfinder to "Charles Evans Hughes, the Great Fault Finder."[59] From Pennsylvania came the advice regarding Vance McCormick "that in my judgment he could do no one thing that will aid more in your election in this campaign than to keep Mr. Hughes on the stump."[60]

As Hughes stumbled, recriminations began among Republicans that focused on Willcox and his management of the campaign. A St. Louis newspaper reported that the nominee had summoned Willcox to that city "and told him, in effect, 'get busy or get out.'" Hughes was reported to be angry at "the series of 'frosts'" on his campaign tour and observers looked for Frank Hitchcock to take over within two weeks.[61] The Republicans countered that the two men "are perfectly satisfied with the existing state of affairs."[62]

In fact, during the first week of September the Republican campaign revived. Hughes got a new, potent issue to use against Wilson, and the party received very encouraging news from Maine when voters went to the polls in that state. The race was on as differences sharpened between the two parties over the always sensitive issue of organized labor and the role of interest groups in the economy. What had begun as a Republican effort to oust Wilson would now become a pitched rhetorical battle over the contrasting ideologies of the two major parties. The two parties began to sound like their modern counterparts.

6 THE CAMPAIGN BECOMES IDEOLOGICAL

President Wilson had a very good month for an incumbent in August 1916. Charles Evans Hughes had revealed himself to be a mediocre candidate on the campaign trail. Still, with the inherent Republican electoral majority in the nation, the flaws of Hughes might not have been decisive if the Democrats had not performed. Wilson respected the ability of the Republican candidate to draw out the votes of his supporters. The president contrasted Hughes with Roosevelt in a spring conversation with Ray Stannard Baker, a popular reporter. "Roosevelt deals in personalities and avoids arguments. One does not need to meet him at all. Hughes is of a very different type. If he is nominated, he will have to be met."[1]

To engage the Republican campaign, the Democrats had by August set up a campaign under Vance McCormick that was functioning with an efficiency that surprised party members who recalled the ineffective organizations of earlier elections in 1904 and 1908. That provided encouraging portents but Wilson himself would have to set his own campaign themes when he gave his acceptance speech. The Democrats looked to their candidate for a performance that would confirm the president's ascendancy over Hughes as an orator.

By 1916 Woodrow Wilson was a very talented speaker. Earlier in the year, his tour of the Middle West and the speeches he delivered there counteracted Democratic opposition to his preparedness program. On May 27, he had spoken to the League to Enforce Peace, where William

Woodrow Wilson.
President Wilson and the Democrats ran an effective reelection campaign that featured the president's biting attacks about the Republicans and the war. Courtesy of the Library of Congress.

Howard Taft was a major player, to enunciate a vision of a postwar world with a "universal association of nations" to "keep the seas open" and to prevent any war that threatened the peace of the world.[2] When Wilson was on his game, he could stir audiences and score points that left his opponents in disarray.

The president and Mrs. Wilson decide to summer at a New Jersey seaside home called "Shadow Lawn" near Long Branch. There on September 2 before an invited audience of Democrats, Wilson formally launched his reelection campaign. At first the proposed location for the speech on the porch of the mansion would have Wilson facing the afternoon sun, but

Wilson's Notification and Acceptance Speech.
When the president launched his campaign on September 2, the Democrats assembled a large crowd at Wilson's summer home, Shadow Lawn, in Long Branch, New Jersey. Courtesy of the Library of Congress.

the organizers moved him "in front of the main door," enabling the president "to be seen by more people—than from any other 'park' location."[3]

After the hoopla of the ceremony had been concluded with the welcoming bands and the festive atmosphere, the president did not strive for oratorical effects since he knew that most Americans would be encountering his speech in their newspapers. Of the Democratic Party, he said "it has merely done its duty. It has merely fulfilled its explicit promises." Unlike the Republicans, Wilson's party had revised the tariff, created the Federal Reserve System, passed the Rural Credits Act, adopted such measures as the Federal Seamen's Act, and implemented an income tax. In sum, in one of the takeaway lines from Wilson's address, "we have in four years come very close to carrying out the platform of the Progressive Party as well as our own; for we are also progressives." Because of that record, to which the Republicans had throughout been opposed, "the Republican party is just the party that *cannot* meet the new conditions of a new age."[4]

Turning to foreign affairs, the president asserted that the United States, in pursuing neutrality, had valued "the fundamental rights of humanity" over property rights. He denounced "the small alien element amongst us which puts loyalty to any foreign power before loyalty to the United States." And he had a dismissive word for those like Hughes "who are making doubtful and conjectural promises of service."[5]

He did not back down before the critics of his Mexican policy. He promised that "the Mexican people are entitled to attempt their liberty from such influences and so long as I have anything to do with the action of our great government I shall do everything in my power to prevent anyone standing in their way."[6]

Of the European War, he maintained that "there must be a just and settled peace, and we here in America must contribute the full force of our enthusiasm and our authority as a nation to the organization of that peace with world-wide foundations." Wilson then reviewed the role of the administration in supporting business enterprise through the Federal Trade Commission, mentioned conservation issues, the needs of labor, and the nation's railroad system. He concluded: "Upon this record and in the faith of this purpose we go to the country."[7]

The president had done what Hughes had failed to do with his acceptance speech. He had framed the issues in a compelling way. Democratic papers were predictably enthusiastic. The *Atlanta Constitution* said, "It is performance and not promise that is going to bring Democratic victory in November." The *Brooklyn Eagle* concluded that "the dominant tone of President Wilson's speech of acceptance is its unquestionable American idealism."[8]

Even the Republicans conceded that his comments made "a strong appeal to a people notably hospitable to altruistic deeds," in the words of the *Philadelphia Public Ledger*.[9] The *Washington Herald*, not friendly to the administration, said the speech would be "recorded as one of the strongest he has ever delivered." The *New York Times* called it "an extraordinarily effective campaign utterance."[10]

As September opened, the Democratic campaign under Vance McCormick's leadership was functioning smoothly in contrast to the highly public struggles of William Willcox and the Republicans. McCormick proved a deft organizer who animated the party headquarters in New York City with energy and common purpose. Few of the usual stories of Democratic infighting made their way into the newspapers. The Democrats had a number of skilled operatives overseeing the various bureaus that sought votes across the country with a zeal not usually seen in the party's campaign organization. Of McCormick, the former football star, he was, according to *Life* magazine, "the head coach for the Democrats, a man who was "rich, able, practiced and husky, and a reformer.'[11] With his subordinates operating in tandem, McCormick supervised an efficient operation. The Democrats were "doing everything we can to get the literature out to the country," wrote one New York worker. The documents had a hard edge with such titles as "Record of Hughes as an Enemy of Labor" and "Mexico. Woodrow Wilson Fights for the Just Rights and the Liberty of an Oppressed and Helpless People." Democratic headquarters reported "getting large orders from all over the North for speeches and we are doing our best to supply everyone at the earliest possible moment." Hugh Wallace told House in late August that "we will gain about 100,000 votes over four years ago from the above nationalities," including French, Jewish, Polish, and Italian voters in New York State. House told Wilson in early October that "the curve during the last few days has been distinctly upward and everybody is increasingly happy around Headquarters."[12]

A particularly effective aspect of the Democratic campaign was the Publicity Bureau, under the direction of Robert Woolley. Beyond the old-style campaign literature Woolley employed newspaper advertising and a series of films to harry Hughes and the Republicans. Woolley made wide use of "He Kept Us out of War" and "He Has Protected Me and Mine" on billboards, street signs, and other media. At the same time, Woolley denounced Theodore Roosevelt and linked Hughes and Roosevelt as war mongers in the popular mind.[13]

A continual constraint on the Democratic campaign was a lack of money. The Republicans had more than they really needed from the business community. The Democrats struggled to obtain contributions from Wilson's rich friends, a few sympathetic business leaders, and the public at large. The declared Democratic total of $1 million trailed the Republican success. A reporter for the London *Times* said it well in his assessment of the election: "the Republicans have lots of cash; the Democrats not much."[14]

The Democrats needed their good organization because it looked like voting blocs they could usually count on were more open to Republican appeals than in previous contests. Irish Americans, ordinarily loyal to Democrats, had been alienated by what they saw as an administration in World War I that tilted toward their ancient enemy, Great Britain. In the short run, the outbreak of the Irish Rebellion sharpened these attitudes. The decision of London to execute the Irish patriot Roger Casement for his ties to the Germans led to charges that the White House had not

Robert Woolley.
Woolley directed the Publicity Bureau of the Wilson campaign with an effectiveness the Republicans had not expected. Courtesy of the Library of Congress.

acted in time to use its influence for clemency toward Casement in the summer of 1916. As an Irish American newspaper observed at the start of the year, even before the rebellion: "If the Democrats desire even a sporting chance at the next election, their policy must be 'Anyone but Wilson.'"[15]

Drawing support from Irish American disaffection but existing in its own right as a source of anti-Democratic feeling was unhappiness with Wilson among Catholics. The president's Mexican policy had involved the belated recognition of the revolutionary leader Venustiano Carranza, whose forces sometimes perpetrated outrages against priests and nuns in his country. Wilson was also supposed to have insulted Catholic leaders by not addressing them by their clerical titles. His appointment of John R. Mott, high up in the Young Men's Christian Association (YMCA), was another source of grievance. Archbishop John Ireland encouraged Hughes to seek the presidency. How much good Democratic countermeasures did to limit the effect of these attacks is hard to determine. Members of a usually reliable voting bloc seemed ready to defect to the GOP candidate. The question was how deep these departures would affect the president's chances.

While the two campaigns were gearing up for the election, an economic crisis was building that confronted Wilson with dangerous political choices. The four railroad brotherhoods were seeking the eight-hour day and time-and-a-half for overtime. The managers of the main railroads rebuffed these requests and requested federal arbitration on June 15. Given the indispensable role of the railroads in the American economy before the advent of airlines and mass ownership of automobiles and trucks, a railroad strike could paralyze the nation. Union members had voted in overwhelming numbers to strike unless the railroads gave way. By mid-August arbitration had failed and a strike loomed.

As the crisis deepened, Wilson threw his personal prestige into the controversy. He summoned both sides to the White House as Theodore Roosevelt had done in the anthracite coal strike fourteen years before in 1902. It became evident that the lines between the two sides were drawn sharply. The railroad presidents insisted that the dispute go to further arbitration, a procedure they believed would enable them to win their case. If that failed, some Republicans asserted that the federal government should seize the railroads, operate them over the protests of the railroad brotherhoods, and in effect break the unions. The unions were having none of it and prepared to strike.

Out of these futile White House talks emerged a conviction in Wilson's mind that the eight-hour day must be adopted to avert a disastrous strike. No friend of unions before he was elected president, Wilson now concluded that the unions were deserving of their core demand. In the days between August 21 and August 28 it became clear that the gap between the two sides was unbridgeable. The prospect of a strike became more real as the unions issued a deadline of September 4.

Wilson went to Congress in person on August 29 where he defended the principle of the eight-hour day and asked for a comprehensive settlement through legislation. He favored expansion of the Interstate Commerce Commission, study of the eight-hour day in practice, the actual adoption of the eight-hour day, and power for the president to assume control of the railroad to assure continuation of service. In the process of his speech he said that "the whole spirit of the time and the preponderant evidence of recent economic experience spoke for the eight-hour day."[16]

Despite vocal congressional approval of Wilson's speech, the lawmakers were cool to the president's package. The White House settled for a simple bill instituting the eight-hour day to avoid the strike. The House endorsed the legislation on September 1, by a vote of 239 to 56, and the

Senate concurred the next day by a closer margin of 43 to 28. Wilson then signed the measure drafted by Representative William C. Adamson and quickly dubbed the Adamson Act, and the immediate strike threat went away. The political response was intense.

The Republicans exploded with rage at what they called a craven presidential surrender to organized labor. An angry Hughes led off the GOP offensive. In speeches in Nashville, Tennessee, and St. Louis, he urged: "Never surrender principle to force." He contended that there should have been a formal investigation of the controversy before the eight-hour bill was enacted. Had Wilson "made instant provision for an inquiry so entirely competent as to command the respect of the country, I am satisfied there could have been no strike." Of course he could not know what the unions would have done, but he was willing to assume that risk. "We have left autocracy. We have left tyranny. We have left force. They shall not come back if we can prevent it."[17] Buoyed by the Maine vote, which he considered "a response to what I said on the Adamson bill," Hughes told Taft, "This is the most shameful proceeding that has come to my attention since I have observed public life and it presents, as it seems to me, a fundamental issue. I propose to press it constantly."[18]

To his Democratic critics, Hughes denied that he was an enemy of labor, citing as did his campaign his pro-labor record as governor to prove his claims. Yet even newspapers that deplored the Adamson Act inquired of Hughes, "What would you have done," as they did about other issues in the campaign. As the controversy developed, a San Francisco newspaper said that a real campaign issue had emerged: "we now have one that grew, like Topsy, and is real flesh and blood." For Republicans, off stride throughout most of the summer, the reaction to the Adamson Act was a tonic. It showed Hughes to advantage. "Which has done most to advance his candidature with the independent citizen," queried the *Wall Street Journal*, "Hughes with his manly utterance at Nashville or Wilson with his cowed and servile Congress?"[19]

In their private correspondence GOP members released their private feelings about the brotherhoods, speaking of "the tyrany [*sic*] of labor unions."[20] Another representative from New York said: "there are worse things than strikes, and one of those things is the destruction of the American system of government." Hughes received congratulations for speaking out "against the sand-bagging of the country by Wilson and the labor unions," and Robert R. McCormick of the *Chicago Tribune* called the Democrats "the most capable fighters at hitting below the belt that have appeared in the political arena for many years."[21] Joseph Hodges Choate, formerly the American ambassador in London under McKinley and Roosevelt, said in a speech at Pittsfield, Massachusetts, on September 5 that Wilson and Congress had "surrendered control of the government for the time being into the hands of men who hold no commission from the people and no right to make their laws."[22] A letter to the editor in the *New-York Tribune* asked: "Have we all been inoculated with the poison of Wilsonism, so that the entire nation is infected with infantile paralysis?"[23]

"As many Republicans see it today, President Wilson and the democratic congressional leaders submitted to the greatest national humiliation of political history" with the enactment of the Adamson law. The GOP prepared to launch a concerted attack in support of Hughes for the rest of the campaign. As the editors of the *New-York Tribune* put it, "to what is shoddy and flabby in current Americanism, Mr. Wilson undoubtedly does appeal."[24] Senator Lawrence Sherman of Illinois told a friend "we have entered a dangerous period of national life. If people do not awake republican government will cease. Class rule will be substituted for popular government." The real issue, wrote one Republican, was "whether the United states [*sic*] Senate was composed of real men or a lot of sniffling cowards who would run at the first word of a loud mouthed bluffer."[25]

But it was not all Republican gain. A Republican editor, recognizing the appeal of the shorter work day, instructed a subordinate to avoid the term "eight hour law" in headlines and to speak only of "the Adamson law." The president of the rail conductors wrote that in thirty days "people will have forgotten the charge that Congress was forced to act and simply remember that the strike was averted."[26] A Republican told Theodore Roosevelt: "Our people are too prosperous at this time, under an existing high tariff and the war credits, to worry themselves over the effect of an eight-hour railroad law with which anyway they have a certain sort of sympathy. Nor can they be got into an excited state of mind about the coercion of Congress."[27]

The most immediate effect was an outpouring of financial support for Hughes and a drying up of contributions for the Democrats. The Republicans now received ample cash from their usual business sympathizers, who felt that Wilson and the Democrats were antibusiness and who had, as the *New-York Tribune* put it, engaged in a "disgraceful surrender to the railroad brotherhoods." One Republican urged William

Willcox to stress the labor issue. "We have nothing therefore to lose and everything to gain by pressing this issue everywhere" since there was nothing "comparable to this truckling surrender of the President and Congress to the threats of the Proletariat" since the days of the French Revolution.[28] The apocalyptic language revealed the depth of Republican frustration about what the president had done.

The passage of the Adamson Act with the beginning of the eight-hour day for railroad workers tapped into some of the most deep-seated fears among Republicans about the existence of class warfare and the prospect of social revolution. Legislating to help a specific group, unless it was the business community in general, was a dangerous and subversive precedent. "We Americans are in one boat," said a Hughes advertisement. "You cannot strike a blow to one group without injury to all."[29] To insist that the railroads pay their employees more through a new law was violating the rules by which capitalism operated for the benefit of everyone. To acknowledge the existence of the rail unions as equal players in the economy was anathema to the leaders and followers within the GOP.

The Wilson administration, in the minds of GOP members, had begun to implement policies that undermined the nature of a free society and thus had to be stopped. The anger of men such as Taft, Roosevelt, and Elihu Root arose from these conclusions. The president was not just a political opponent. He represented a dangerous force that was tearing at the fabric of society. Wilson did not have "the spirit of American nationality" because he was a Democrat. He pushed for the Adamson law because Wilson had behind him only "fine words" and "skillful argument," said Root, not the Republican values, which had always been "national to the core."[30] The Democrats, southern and sectional, lacked the true national perspective that had always been the special property of the Republicans. The Republicans and Democrats were taking up policy positions that would characterize their rivalry for the remainder of the century.

There was, however, a further downside to the emphasis that Hughes placed on the alleged iniquity of the Adamson Act. If this was the defining issue between the two parties what did that say about the earlier criticism of the Republican candidate about the performance of the administration? What did it tell the voters about Hughes if, after leaving the Supreme Court, it was only several months later that he discovered the Adamson Act as a virtual rationale for his candidacy?

During the first week of September, criticism of Hughes persisted within the Republican network. "The Republican campaign keeps staggering on. As yet Mr. Hughes has created no enthusiasm and his management remains execrable."[31] After a Hughes rally in St. Louis on September 2, a Republican concluded: "For instance the meeting here last night was organized for cheering purposes. The crowd yelled for twenty-one minutes when he appeared on the platform, but the cheering had practically all died out by the time he had spoken twenty minutes."[32]

These qualms were swept aside when the state of Maine voted at the end of the first week of September in what politicians of both parties had come to regard as a reliable predictor of the eventual national result. When Maine voted it recorded a thumping majority for Hughes and the Republicans, some 13,000 votes ahead of the Democrats. It looked to pundits as if the appeal of protection and Americanism was working after all. The *New-York Tribune* headlined "Hughes Sees Vindication in Maine Result." As Hughes informed Theodore Roosevelt, "after the result in Maine I think we have good reason to be cheerful."[33]

In a sense, Hughes learned the wrong lesson from the Maine voting. Newspapers reported that "the Republican nominee is satisfied with the work of Mr. Willcox; he is also satisfied that the campaign he is making is a winning one." Of the trouble spots in the West, he was heedless of the signs that Kansas was in doubt and Wilson strong in Ohio and also of the bad impression he had made with Progressives in California. Hughes thought that when Hiram Johnson won the Republican primary the congratulatory telegram he had sent would patch things up and therefore "the nomination of Governor Johnson by California Republicans clears up the situation in that state."[34] He had no inkling of how much his presence at the luncheon served by "scab" waiters had alienated union voters in the San Francisco area.

So Republican confidence in the predictive power of Maine returned and the warning signs in the country were ignored or played down. It was thought that one element in the Hughes victory in Maine had been a very belligerent speech that Roosevelt made for him in Lewiston in the days leading up to the balloting. Roosevelt hit hard. The president was "worse than Pontius Pilate," the Mexican policy had been a "murderous peace," and overall "it would be a grave misfortune for the people of the United States to re-elect Mr. Wilson." Roosevelt also attacked the loyalty of German Americans.[35]

To defeat the hated Wilson and restore the natural order of American politics with a Republican victory, Hughes decided that a visible reconciliation of Roosevelt and Taft would symbolize that process of reunion. If the two men, who had met briefly in 1915, could be seen to have gotten over their past differences, it would send a positive message to Republicans and independents everywhere of the party's strong chances.

Hughes bent his personal charm during September to staging such a moment. The occasion was arranged for October 3 at the Union League Club in New York City, a bastion of upper-class Republicanism. There it was hoped that Roosevelt and Taft would meet and exchange a few pro-Hughes words in a tangible public demonstration that all Republicans were behind the national ticket.

When it happened, Republican newspapers gushed with enthusiasm at the significance of the episode. The only problem was, while the two men shook hands, they said not a word to each other. It was another awkward incident for the Hughes camp. The former presidents sat at different tables during the speeches. The three men did speak to the audience of invited Republicans. Taft said, "we are holding one of those exceptional meetings of the ex-Presidential club. It is not a large membership. And the members do not always, or perhaps ever, entertain completely harmonious views." He compared 1916 to 1896 and asked: "Is the treatment that we have given to Mexico one that assures us peace?"[36]

Hughes responded to the emerging Democratic contention that a Republican victory would mean war. "We have heard in recent days that the alternative of the policy of the present administration is war. I think the alternative of the policy of the present administration is peace with honor." He charged that "we have been living through a period of national humiliation."[37] How the country might achieve peace with honor without going to war Hughes did not say.

Roosevelt also spoke with characteristic vigor against Wilson. He called the sinking of the *Lusitania* "murder on the high sea" and said of Wilson "no man has the right to claim kinship with Abraham Lincoln if he is too proud to fight." He added that "Mr. Wilson is praised for the most part by people with shoulders that slope like champagne bottles," reminiscent of the slurs against those men in the Gilded Age who lacked the broad shoulders that denoted true masculine virtue.[38] He also took a shot at hyphenated Americans.

Never a team player, Roosevelt refused to adjust his behavior to the needs of the nominee. He had earlier vetoed the use of moving pictures of Republicans, including Willcox, making a symbolic visit to his home at Oyster Bay. He did not want his image used "in any moving picture of a fictitious type. That would be both undignified and improper."[39] Roosevelt's qualms extended to refusing to have his likeness used on a political button showing himself, Taft, and Hughes together.[40]

It was as if Roosevelt were running the campaign and Hughes was one of his subordinates. On the eve of the Maine election, the *New-York Tribune* ran a front-page story about how "Colonel Roosevelt has taken a firm grip on the reins of the Republican Presidential Campaign." Worried about the progress of the canvass and "not as optimistic about the outcome as some of those enthusiasts who prate about roseate prospects," Roosevelt saw a hard fight still ahead and was bent on a policy to "'loosen up' and get into the battle."[41]

To the extent that Hughes encouraged Roosevelt, still the most charismatic Republican, in this course, he was making a crucial error. Roosevelt's bellicose and strident language identified the Republicans with a warlike posture on the neutrality issue and confirmed the Democratic argument in favor of Wilson's more peaceful approach. For Roosevelt held nothing back in his rhetorical assault on Wilson's performance. In a speech in Battle Creek, Michigan, on September 30, he described the president as cowardly with "a positive genius for striking when the iron is cold and fearing to strike when the iron is hot."[42]

Following the Union League meeting, Roosevelt expanded the number of speeches to which he had committed himself for the Hughes campaign. Roosevelt took to the stump in a rolling series of appearances indicting the president. He and Hughes planned to spend time in Kentucky where Chairman Willcox said the Republicans had "an excellent chance" to carry that border state.[43] Roosevelt attracted large crowds in the state as he accused Wilson of following toward Germany "the course of dishonor, of temporary safety, and of permanent danger."[44]

As Gus Karger observed in mid-October, "Roosevelt is stirring up the animals, but he has done M. Hughes no good since first he went into the Maine campaign. He may be helping him in certain directions, but he has certainly succeeded in irritating the German-Americans practically to the breaking point. For every German-American vote that goes to Wilson that gentleman ought to send M. Roosevelt a personal letter of thanks."[45]

Sharing the optimism of his colleagues, living in a cocoon as a candidate, Hughes missed the warning signs that some Republicans sought to bring to his attention. Though the campaign staff was large, even bloated, there never was an efficient process for preparing diverse speeches and statements for the candidate. As a result, Hughes became repetitive and that diminished newspaper coverage of his daily activities. Large audiences cheered him on the spot, but his overall message did not get out and resonate with the public. As Gus Karger told former president Taft, Hughes lacked many of the qualities of an effective orator. When heckled he came alive, but only then. President Wilson told a friend about his rival, "I am inclined to follow the course suggested by a friend of mine who says that he had always followed the rule never to murder a man who is committing suicide and clearly this man is committing suicide slowly but surely."

Hughes received ample warning that he could not rely on a single speech, delivered over and over, but needed three or four "to secure a maximum of publicity." Colonel Robert R. McCormick of the *Chicago Tribune* wrote him in early October to say that "the public is far from understanding thoroughly the issues of this campaign. I think you owe it to them and to yourself to get your position on the various questions in deliberate length on paper."[46]

That the problem persisted is evident from a document in the Hughes Papers. On October 18, Henry L. Stimson, George W. Wickersham, and Frank Vanderlip sent Hughes a memorandum that claimed "the candidate of the Republican Party has not been effectively presented to the American people." His speeches had not been prepared in advance "and sent throughout the country to be released simultaneously at the time they are delivered." That failing prevented friendly editors from writing "supporting editorials and to take out the telling points in the speech, box them and place them where the eye of the average reader can be guided to them."

The outcome was that the message Hughes was trying to deliver was eluding the electorate. The writers of the letter warned, "the result has been a decided slump in the Republican campaign and a tendency in voters to turn toward Wilson." They told the candidate that readers of newspapers "can't and won't read the same speech over and over each day and the newspaper editors must have something to feature and time enough in which to do it."[47]

The candidate did not take such advice. He adhered to the broad themes of his acceptance speech and stressed the tariff right through to the end of the campaign. As William Allen White later observed, "he talked tariff like Mark Hanna. He talked of industrial affairs like McKinley." For all the high expectations that accompanied the nomination of Hughes, he failed to meet them, and a tangible sense of disappointment is evident in the remarks of those who had looked to Hughes with hope in May and June. "Mr. Hughes is not doing himself justice in this campaign that he has a fresher and more penetrating mind than his speeches reveal."[48]

Hughes had shown his intellectual ability on the Supreme Court. If he now emphasized the tariff as his major domestic policy in 1916, it was because that was what at heart he believed. Coming to political maturity in the Gilded Age during the heyday of the Republican protectionism of James G. Blaine and William McKinley, he shared their conviction that high tariffs represented a true American policy that embodied national values. These themes had united Republicans before and now would again.

Progressives might regard the tariff as a relic of an older political system but Hughes did not. "If you study the signs of the times," he said, "the economic conditions of our life, you know very well you have to meet this condition by an intelligent, sane application of the Republican doctrine of protection to American industry." To Hughes, the prospect of American workers facing European products that low-wage workers on that continent had created was a key question. "The simple proposition is presented. Shall we lower American wages or shall we protect American wages." The tariff was necessary to stave off postwar challenges and beneficial because it benefitted all elements of society and thus avoided the social conflict that Hughes deplored. He rebuked "any suggestion of classes, of class war for class interests. There is no hope for us if we have that notion of American life."[49]

To keep his uneasy coalition of progressives and conservatives together against Wilson and the Democrats, Hughes saw the tariff as a reliable winning issue. He had been either governor or on the Supreme Court in the quarrels over the Payne-Aldrich law of 1909 and Canadian Reciprocity in 1910–1911. Nor did he have any part in the Underwood Tariff law of 1913, though he could denounce the hard times in 1913–1914 at great length. If the tariff seemed old hat to some who heard him, Hughes did not care. It was real to him, and consonant with a campaign that said: "It is the lofty, patriotic ideal that must beckon us on and to which we must be faithful." Again he deplored "every thing that seems intended to set one group against another group, that seems intended to foster one interest at the expense of another interest."[50] From his perspective, the tariff, as Republicans had wielded it for generations, could once again restore national unity and economic cohesion. At bottom, Hughes was correct that the two parties offered different visions of the American future. The Democrats wanted to address the specific questions facing workers, farmers, business leaders, and women. The Republicans saw that as class warfare and from it they recoiled.

Convinced as the Republicans were that Wilson was unworthy to lead the nation because of the flaws in his personal character, they readily circulated the personal attacks that were very current in 1916, going back to the 1912 election. There is no evidence that Hughes knew or condoned such tactics. He never mentioned Wilson by name in his daily speeches though he seems to have had little respect for his opponent, but he would not have stooped to a personal assault.

Wilson had sometimes verged on recklessness in his personal life. While he was still president of Princeton University, he had vacationed without his wife, Ellen, in Bermuda where he fell under the spell of a woman named Mary Hulbert Peck. The exact extent of their romantic involvement remains in doubt. Wilson biographers disagree whether the couple had a physical relationship but at the very least Wilson had written her some passionate letters and loaned her some money in actions that would be hard to defend in public.

The rumors about the Wilson-Peck involvement had been around four years earlier and Theodore Roosevelt had brushed them off as implausible and unlikely to be credited.[51] Now Roosevelt was willing to believe the worst about the president. He made a passing allusion to Wilson's ability to get away with such behavior. Others who spread the stories asked whether the president had been faithful to his marriage vows and was therefore morally upright in his office. References to "Peck's Bad Boy," a juvenile novel, circulated widely in Republican circles. Inevitably, friends of the Wilsons asked him about the stories and so he learned what his political enemies were saying. Wilson felt even more aggrieved about how his character was being portrayed.

Another canard involved the physical condition of the grave of his first wife in Georgia. Tales circulated that the burial site had been neglected. The one-time Populist, Tom Watson, gave the story great currency in his newspaper. Steps had been taken to prepare a proper memorial for the deceased Ellen Wilson, and the president bridled at the allegations that he was spending lavishly on his second wife while neglecting the final resting place of his first wife. As he told Tumulty, "Please say to these people that this is just a case of the basest and grossest calumny. "Mrs. Wilson's grave is being kept in the most loving and careful manner."[52]

Other allegations charged that former president Grover Cleveland had criticized Wilson's record as president of Princeton and that Wilson had mismanaged funds at the institution during his administration. Friends of Wilson at Princeton and even some of his former adversaries denied these allegations.

Taking notice of these smears would only have given them more currency, and yet a defense of the president as a private citizen seemed imperative. In this instance Colonel House had the proper answer. He suggested that Stockton Axson, the former brother-in-law of the president, prepare an article on the president's home life. The resulting document, published in the *New York Times*, along with a presidential interview with the former muckraker Ida Tarbell, provided Democratic counters to the Republican whispering campaign. Axson was mawkish in what was essentially a valentine to his former brother-in-law, but it may have swayed a few voters hearing the many lurid stories about the president that circulated.[53]

The existence of Republican slurs on the president's character got back to Wilson and intensified his existing bitterness against Hughes and his party. These feelings carried over into the post-election and led Wilson later to write: "The campaign was indeed one of the most virulent and bitter and, I must say, one of the most unfair on the part of the Republican opposition that the country has ever seen."[54] The president would not forget how he had been traduced by his partisan attackers. In that spirit the campaign of 1916 lurched into its closing weeks with intense feelings of animosity on both sides. It would get worse before the voters made their decision.

7
THE FINAL MONTH

As the presidential campaign entered the final month, the candidates had stirred some popular interest without relying on the organized canvassing of an earlier time in national politics. The two parties used crude movies and extensive newspaper advertising to convey their messages to the electorate. Two observers of the process concluded "the political education and persuasion that is now necessary is far more expensive than the coercion and vote-buying by which elections used to be carried."[1]

As prognosticators sized up the potential result, the Republicans seemed to be dominant in the Northeast, but the West was the contested battleground where a close result was expected. After a Democratic survey of national voter sentiment was given to him, Colonel House was told that "while the condition was very close, there is ample favorable sentiment to re-elect the president."[2]

Following his well-received acceptance speech, the president had become more active in his own behalf, engaging the points that Hughes was presenting against his record. On September 8 he went to Atlantic City and spoke to the meeting of the National American Woman Suffrage Association. While he did not change his position on the national amendment, he gave the audience the positive assurances that this more moderate group was anxious to hear about their cause. "The tide is rising to meet the moon, you need not be afraid that it will not come to its flood," he told them. That was enough for some women to offset to some degree the Hughes endorsement of the national amendment.[3]

Then on September 23 in a speech at Shadow Lawn he defended the eight-hour day and the Adamson Act.[4] A week later he delivered a telling blow against Hughes and also Roosevelt. Speaking to Young Democrats, he said that the Republicans were promising to change foreign policy. "There is only one choice against peace and that is war." Many leading Republicans, by which he meant Roosevelt, were speaking out for a more aggressive foreign policy and therefore "the certain prospect of the success of the Republican party is that we shall be drawn in one form or another into the embroilments of the European War." In addition, he warned, the force of the United States "will be used to produce in Mexico the kind of law and order which some American investors in Mexico consider most to their advantage."[5] That is, calm would be established in a way that would work against the broad mass of the Mexican people.

The Democratic theme that had been in gestation since the national convention now came fully into view. The national committee announced through the New York *World* that the campaign slogan for the party would be "Wilson and Peace or Hughes and War." Vance McCormick told the paper that what the president had said "defines the paramount issue of the campaign." Chairman Willcox accused the president of threatening the country with war in response, but the Republicans knew that the formulation of the question in this way hurt their overall chances.[6]

The suggestion that Republican victory would mean war stung and put Hughes on the defensive. In Nebraska he proclaimed, "I am a man of peace. Who wants war? I don't want war."[7] His denials reminded his listeners of how he differed from the president on foreign policy. What did peace with honor mean if it did not involve a stronger posture toward the Germans than Wilson adopted and would not that course risk war? And then there was Roosevelt. He was out attacking German Americans for their disloyalty and the president for not seizing German ships and provoking a confrontation. What role would Roosevelt have in a Hughes administration and how much influence would he have with a new president? Rumors circulated that Roosevelt would be named secretary of state with war the next step.

Demonstrating the potential effect of the war on the United States was the appearance of the trans-Atlantic German submarine U-53 off the East Coast in early October. The vessel opened itself up for tours by curious Americans and then returned to its military mission of sinking Allied shipping. Headlines in the New York newspapers greeted the U-53, and the resulting furor led Wilson to reassure the public that the Sussex Pledge still operated. The episode passed from the scene without a confrontation, but it illustrated how much the Democratic campaign depended on the tacit agreement of the German government to keep things quiet. As Wilson told the German ambassador, "the president feared that a carrying on of the U-Boat war along the American coast would bring such excitement of public opinion on this side with regard to the election that he would not be able to control it."[8] The Germans took heed, as did the British and French with their naval vessels, the submarine scare subsided, and the campaign continued.

Mexico, too, remained dormant as an issue through October 1916. The American punitive expedition under Pershing was still in Mexico, but Wilson saw to it that no military action occurred while talks went on with Mexican officials about an eventual withdrawal of Pershing's troops. The negotiations went nowhere for weeks, but neither did violence erupt to undercut the president's reelection. Hughes and Roosevelt pressed for further action toward Mexico and their stance cost them many votes in the West. Anxiety about war with Mexico was as powerful in the West as were apprehensions about future involvement in Europe. Republicans failed to perceive just how deep voter resistance to expanded involvement in military action in Mexico ran in the West.

A dramatic moment in the campaign came on October 1. In the New Jersey Democratic primary incumbent Senator James Martine, no friend of the president, had won renomination over a pro-Wilson candidate. In New York a Republican representative ran in the Democratic primary and won 36 percent of the vote. Anti-Wilson partisans in the Irish community thought they saw an opening to mock the president. In the wake of these results, Jeremiah A. O'Leary of the American Truth Society, an organization with close ties to Irish patriots and full of anti-British sympathies, sent Wilson a telegram that complained of the president's "leniency with the British Empire, your approval of war loans, the ammunition traffic," and then asked Wilson when he would "respond to these evidences of popular disapproval of your policies by action?" It was meant to provoke a White House answer, but O'Leary got more than he expected.

Wilson fired back at once in a peremptory telegram. "I would feel deeply mortified to have you or anybody like you vote for me. Since you have access to many disloyal Americans and I have not I will ask you to convey this message to them." The testy exchange naturally produced extensive newspaper coverage in the days that followed.[9]

Colonel House wrote the president that "your telegram to O'Leary is the best thing so far in the campaign and will do more good than you can realize."[10] Historians have generally shared this verdict and considered the wire a presidential win. However, Republican reporter Gus Karger took a different view. Wilson "gained nothing by taking notice of O'Leary's message," he wrote to Taft. It was not a turning point, as House surmised, but only one of the several flaps that characterized October 1916.[11]

Ever since the nomination of Hughes, there had been talk that he had given secret assurances about his foreign policy views in exchange for German American electoral support. The Democrats hoped to establish a direct connection. The party found documents showing that Hughes in September had met with prominent German Americans and told them that he favored "the absolute protection of American lives and American property and American commerce." His words to his potential supporters matched what he was saying in public and did not change many votes that were not already committed to one candidate or another. However, the talk that Hughes was cozy with the German Americans would not go away. A resident of North Dakota informed Roosevelt that German Americans in his state "look to Hughes, when he is elected to deal gently with Germany." Another friend of Roosevelt from Indiana told him, "There has been a growing impression with me that Hughes is not frank on the German question."[12]

One striking aspect of the campaign was the heightened role of women on the side of Charles Evans Hughes through a special campaign train that took progressive and wealthy women supporters of the Republican candidate across the country. Frances Kellor, a prominent reformer who had worked with Roosevelt in the Progressive Party, was a driving force behind the project, which she later described as "a big courageous national experiment bent upon a mission of nationalism, carrying neighbors and friends of Mr. Hughes to interpret his record to the United States."[13]

On October 2, a special eight-car train left Grand Central Station in New York City with a cadre of women soon labeled the "Hughesettes." The object of the train was to transport well-known progressive women

Frances Kellor.
A progressive reformer who supported Hughes, Frances Kellor campaigned with other women on a special train that toured the West amid Democratic heckling and protests. Courtesy of the Library of Congress.

across the country to explain why they were supporting Hughes and the Republicans. They set out first to Albany and Buffalo, went through the Middle West, and thence across the continent to the Pacific Coast. The membership of the experiment in surrogacy included some distinguished figures, including Mary Antin, a prominent writer, Maude Howe Elliott, daughter of Julia Ward Howe, and Frances Kellor. The trip was underwritten by some wealthy and prominent society women, including Mrs. John Hay Whitney and the wife of one of the Guggenheims. That contributed to the impression that these affluent women were out to tell their less well-heeled sisters how to vote. The trip had been under way but a week when former Indiana senator Albert J. Beveridge wrote his own wife: "The special is hurting Hughes terribly. Handbills scattered everywhere about the 'Billionaires Special' giving names of heavy guarantors like Mrs. Guggenheim, Mrs. Vanderbilt, Mrs. Whitney, etc."[14]

Other challenges followed. At Portland, Oregon, women chanting "Wilson! We want Wilson" appeared as the Hughesettes left their train for the hotel. And the number of Wilson females outnumbered the Re-

Newton Baker. Secretary of War Newton Baker caused a political flap when he allegedly compared Mexican revolutionaries to the soldiers of the American Revolution. Republicans denounced his statement as unpatriotic. Courtesy of the Library of Congress.

publican women 8 to 1 on this occasion with banners that read "which goose laid the Hughes special golden eggs?" In Chicago the women had eggs thrown at them by angry Wilson supporters.[15] On balance, the women's special did the Hughes cause little good and by emphasizing the affluent background of the women may have hurt the candidate's cause.

With the election shaping up to be very close, both sides magnified any slip by the opposition. On October 16, Secretary of War Newton D. Baker seemed to provide the Republicans with an opening. Picked in early 1916 after Lindley M. Garrison resigned, Baker had a pacifist background that to Republicans made him ill suited to carry on the work of getting the nation ready for war. According to the report in the *New-York Tribune*, which usually gave Democrats the worst in their reporting, Baker had compared the actions of Mexican rebels to the behavior of soldiers in the Continental Army in the darkest days of the revolution under George Washington. Baker was quoted in the *Tribune*'s version of his speech as saying, "Washington's soldiers in the march to Valley Forge stole everything they could lay their hands on; took the silver vessels out of the churches and sold them to buy drink. They drove ministers out of the churches. Their money was worthless and they were just as bad character as the Mexicans."[16]

The next day, the *Tribune* reported that a swelling volume of protests against what it termed "Baker's Slurs" had come "from far and near."[17] The Empire State Society of the Sons of the American Revolution condemned "in strongest terms the unpatriotic language of the Secretary of War." A resident of Pittsburgh informed Baker that "If Patriotism means anything to a citizen-by-birth of this Nation—then *The utterance of yourself and the silence of the Administration* in whose official family you are—*is nothing short of Treason*, morally if not legally."[18]

On October 19, speaking at Youngstown, Ohio, the scene of his 1908 triumph, Hughes told the crowd: "I never supposed that the day would come when a representative of an American Administration would say that about the men who gave us our liberty."[19] By October 23 patriotic societies of women chimed in, calling Baker "a man of such amazing ignorance of history and so lacking in ideals" that he was "not a fit head for the Army of the United States and would tend seriously to injure its morale."[20] In North Dakota, the Republicans ran an advertisement about Baker's speech that called his comments an example of the INDIFFERENCE and the DUPLICITY of the Wilson administration. The ad charged that "Americans want a patriotic American who will name a patriotic American cabinet."[21]

By October 26, Baker issued a statement through the Democratic National Committee denying that he had ever said that Washington's soldiers "had stolen silver out of the churches." He could not recall his exact words but he remembered he had said that Washington's men "were the brave founders of our liberties."[22] Baker's denial removed some of the fuel from the episode, which faded away in the closing days of the canvass. The Republicans had made as much of Baker's apparent gaffe as they could and yet never elicited a response from Wilson. But in the heated atmosphere of 1916 a further charge against the president's honesty soon took the focus to another aspect of Wilson's record.

Henry Cabot Lodge, whose hatred of Wilson now bordered on the pathological, said in a biting speech in Brockton, Massachusetts, on October 26 that he had conclusive proof of Wilson's double dealing. He charged that the president had been duplicitous in his handling of the diplomatic crisis with Germany that followed the sinking of the *Lusitania* in May 1915. Specifically, Lodge alleged that the president had in his second note to the German government added a postscript that assured Berlin not to worry about the strong wording of the first *Lusitania* note because the whole matter could be submitted to arbitration. If true, this was political dynamite that would reveal Wilson to be tricky and dishonest.[23]

The Wilson administration denied the truth of Lodge's charges and the president himself, in answer to a query from a member of the public, wrote that "the statement made by Senator Lodge is untrue."[24] He said he had not made any postscript or amendment of the *Lusitania* note. As was sometimes the case with Wilson, his unequivocal statement was an example of his practice of "grazing the truth." There was a draft press release prepared at the time that did what Lodge charged and Wilson had decided not to issue it after there were objections from the cabinet. In that era, questioning the word of the president was simply not done. As a result, Lodge, however, had to swallow what Wilson had said, albeit with reluctance, since he knew from Lindley M. Garrison and others that the president was lying. For the senator it was yet another example of the duplicity of the president. Relations between the two men, never good, now reached acute levels of toxicity that carried forward into the future.

In the closing days of the canvassing, the issue of race, which had not featured much in the national back-and-forth between the parties, bubbled up on the front pages of the newspapers. The Justice Department sent out warnings of a great migration of southern blacks into Middle Western states to turn these battleground contests to the Republicans by alleged voter fraud and illegal voting. Federal district attorneys in the region received directives to be on the alert for such criminal election tactics. The attorney general, Thomas Watt Gregory, "has ordered a special inquiry into complaints that colored men are being sent in great numbers to doubtful States under promise of work at high wages."[25]

Up to that time, neither of the two major parties had made much effort to attract the black vote in the North. Assuming that the segregationist policies of the Wilson White House had alienated African American voters, the Republicans had done no more than include an article attacking Wilson and the Democrats in their campaign textbook.[26]

In view of the low esteem in which African Americans held President Wilson by 1916 because of his racial policies, it might have seemed logical for Hughes to have made inroads among black voters. The former New York governor, however, had not been a notable friend of black Americans in Albany. As governor, "he did not make good on solitary colored appointment, big or little." To repeated requests for a black appointee, Hughes had replied that he would not appoint any man because he was colored, Irish, German, or what-not. As one black leader noted, "usually that high idealistic attitude results in the utter ignoring of Ham."[27] So it was with Hughes. With no reference to black issues in the GOP platform, the whole question boiled down to "since we know that nothing can be expected of Mr. Wilson, all we can do is to support Hughes and trust to luck as to what he would say or do."[28]

Unlike 1912, when Wilson had demonstrated a willingness to woo the black vote, the president was quiet on race in 1916. There is a letter in the Thomas J. Walsh Papers where Robert S. Hudspeth, a longtime Democratic worker and chair of the Labor Bureau of the national Democratic campaign, reported that "under instructions from Chairman McCormick I am forming a bureau here to have charge of negro voters." The goal was "to go ahead and create the Bureau so that the negroes would see that the democrats have not ignored them." Hudspeth proposed "to secure a headquarters, designate three influential and intelligent colored men to take charge," provide them with a "small clerical force, and feel that they are doing something."[29] He wanted to have the bureau at work by September 1. How much Hudspeth's operation did beyond publishing a single campaign flyer is not clear, but blacks remained skeptical. One black Democrat told the president's secretary of having heard colleagues say, "any colored man who tells you he'll vote for Wilson is a liar."[30]

Then, three weeks before the election, news of warnings from the Justice Department of as many as 60,000 black men leaving the South for the Middle West perhaps to vote in November began popping up in newspapers. There was a genuine shift of population of blacks out of the South. It was part of the Great Migration of African Americans from the South to northern cities during the twentieth century. Unable to endure the daily humiliations of the racist South and drawn by the urgent demand for labor that war contracts produced in the North, those blacks who were able to escape from southern states began to flee northward. Stories appeared in metropolitan newspapers in 1916 marking the extent of the population shift and its implications.[31]

These accounts had a certain alarmist emphasis as though blacks were being driven by irrational forces in a search for better jobs and better employment. There was also the implication that African Americans belonged in the South performing their historic roles as field hands and agricultural laborers. It was, read a headline in the *New-York Tribune* in October 1916, "an alarming migration of Negro labor. The Department of Labor was receiving such "alarming reports" and had instructed officials "to discourage this movement." It blamed "prison employment agencies" over which it had "no control" for the trend. In some southern states, laws had been enacted "forbidding the solicitation of laborers to work outside the state unless a license is obtained from the state authorities."[32]

With the proximity to the election, some officials in the Justice Department believed that partisan politics were also at work. Could these black men be on the move to perpetrate voting frauds in key northern states such as Indiana and Illinois? Would the Republicans wield the black vote in this election as southerners were convinced they had done years before in Reconstruction? There were those in the Wilson administration who thought that such a result was a possibility and they acted to alert the public to the danger. Thomas Watt Gregory was Wilson's second attorney general appointed after his predecessor James McReynolds went on the Supreme Court in 1914. A graduate of the University of Texas and a close ally of Colonel Edward M. House, Gregory believed in, as he later wrote to William G. McAdoo in 1928, "the continuous efforts of the Republican party since the Civil War to force upon the south negro equality and destroy the culture and civilization of our fathers."[33]

That there was concern at the highest levels of the administration is evident from a letter that Assistant Attorney General Samuel J. Graham sent to the president on October 20. Graham had recently been in Ohio, Indiana, and Michigan and he warned Wilson of a corrupt Republican scheme to carry the election in the Middle West through various illicit procedures—"colonization, false registration and voting, repeating counting where they have control of the election machinery, etc." Graham offered to meet with Wilson to outline the nature of Republican wrongdoing.[34]

When the Justice Department began receiving reports of the movements of black men from South to North, Gregory smelled an electoral rat. He shared Graham's verdict that the Republican leaders were capable of anything. Instructions went out to district attorneys in the Middle West to be on the alert for evidence of suspicious behavior at the polls. The *Washington Post* reported that "Attorney General Gregory, in addition to general instructions recently given to federal district attorneys in advance of the election" had "ordered a special inquiry into complaints that colored men are being sent in great numbers to doubtful states under promises of work at high wages."[35]

The Justice Department alleged that it had information "that within the last three months approximately 60,000 negroes have been transported from certain Southern States to Northern and Western States mainly to Middle Western states, particularly Ohio, Indiana and Illinois." Worse yet was the fact that "a number of these negroes have registered in violation of the laws of the States to which they have gone and have expressed the intention of voting in those states."[36]

As Elliott Rudwick showed a half-century ago, a particular focus for the widespread reports of black colonization and subsequent voting fraud was East St. Louis, Illinois, in the southern part of the state. Democrats wanted to prevent Representative William Rodenberg from regaining the seat he had held from 1903 to 1913. Rodenberg was broadly sympathetic to blacks in the district and doled out patronage plums accordingly. Local Democratic newspapers warned of the presence of "Rodenberg Black Belt Colonists" and one sheriff, a Democrat, said that he had received letters warning him of "bad niggers" coming from Tennessee."[37]

All the Democratic alarmism about the prospect of fraud through black voters in the Middle West was finally too much for the leaders of the Republican campaign. Through Representative Thomas Miller of Delaware, the party's congressional campaign committee called the administration's charges "too preposterous for answer." Miller asserted that circumstances "brand the story as false and as a means to deceive the voters of the country in the closing hours of the campaign." Pointing out the logistical problems the Republicans would have confronted had they endeavored to relocate 60,000 black men from the South, Miller added that "it looks like another attempt to use the executive department for partisan purposes, for if the Department of Justice had such information as they claim to have about this matter, why did they wait until the closing hours of the campaign to spring something which cannot be proved, but which they know can probably be used to the detriment of the Republican party, untrue as it may be?"[38]

Nothing ever materialized to show the validity of the fears of the Justice Department. Illinois and Indiana would go Republican in the election without reliance on black votes, while the Democrats would carry the key state of Ohio. The main impact seems to have been to raise racial tensions in East St. Louis in a foreshadowing of the devastating riot there the following summer. The episode also likely stoked animosities between the blacks and whites in that city.

The final weeks of the campaign saw Wilson engaged in an active way with leadership of his own reelection effort. Gone were thoughts of a few addresses at Shadow Lawn to friendly audiences. Gone, too, was the tradition that it was unseemly for an incumbent president to involve himself in a direct way for reelection. Wilson was in it to win as the only secure path to achieve another four years in the White House. After 1916 presidents went on the hustings in reelection campaigns.

On October 16, speaking to Wilson volunteers composed of leading progressives, he said that the Republicans had three goals: first, to oust the comptroller of the currency to prevent him from making banks obey the law; second, to gain control of the new banking system; and third, to obtain military support "back of their financial enterprises in Mexico" and the rest of the world. Democratic government would be replaced "by men who have no public objects except the objects of spoliation." As a result, the choice confronting the voters was between the public interest and "the interest of certain privately controlled and secretly concerning interest."[39]

To the warnings that Hughes was giving about the dangers to American workers from European competition when the war ended, Wilson said, "I wonder how any thinking man can entertain an opinion of that sort. It is obviously based upon singular and profound ignorance." Since Hughes had been saying that since his acceptance speech, Wilson, in the most polite and elevated language, was calling his rival a fool.[40] At Shadow Lawn on October 28 he said "the forces of the opposition are confused" and the Republicans had mastered "the art of talking without saying anything." The Democrats, on the other hand had a "definite and settled policy of self-respecting peace." For Wilson, the Republicans had revealed their true selves in their continuing emphasis in the speeches of Hughes about the protective tariff. Their position was, as Wilson put it, "we have got to have protection on the old lines and in the old familiar right away."[41] Therefore, Wilson concluded in his final campaign speech in New Jersey, the real difference between the Republicans and Democrats was what they put before the American people: "the Republican party offers them masters; we offer them comrades and leaders."

By the end of the campaign Wilson had lost all respect for his opponent. He told an interviewer that "I have such utter contempt for Mr. Hughes now that I don't want to pay him the compliment of referring to him, he has sunk so low." The president added that "the Republican party stands now for the things it stood for under Mark Hanna. There is no such thing as progressive Republicans."[42] In the election Wilson considered "we are to decide whether we will resume government under guardians or continue government by public opinion."

While the Democrats knew the election would be close, they looked to the voting with confidence. Meanwhile, the Republicans had abandoned the swagger and over-confidence of the earlier months. Nicholas Murray Butler, while hopeful that Hughes would win, believed "every possible mistake has been made at National Committee headquarters, and if Hughes is elected despite all it would be something of a miracle." A Republican operative on the scene in Missouri now summed up the Democratic appeal as "Peace" and "Prosperity."[43]

It is not clear how much Republicans were aware of what was happening on the ground in key states. Hughes later wrote that he had little idea of peace sentiments in normally Republican Kansas until election day when the state went for Wilson.[44] In California there was no follow-up to make sure the Hiram Johnson Progressives were delivering the vote. In many areas of California the usual Republican campaign simply did not exist in October as the Johnson forces concentrated on the senatorial contest. The state of things in Ohio was problematic where the prohibition issue was cutting against Hughes and labor was getting out Wilson ballots. Matters looked so positive in Eastern states that the situation in the West, except in Michigan, escaped Republican notice. Hughes did some last-minute campaigning in Michigan that he later credited with keeping the state for the Republicans.

Hughes in the closing days continued along the thematic lines he had already laid out. In Boston on October 26, he said, "If I am elected, as I expect to be, we shall have an American administration with exclusively American policies, devoted to American interests. I propose to be an American President, unswerved by any suggestion of foreign influence." The ways in which Wilson had served other than American interests Hughes did not say. He charged instead that the Wilson government had put this nation in four years on the road to class war to a greater degree than had been accomplished in the preceding generation. Hughes was speaking to and evoking the traditional Republican doubts about the essential lack of legitimacy that party members attributed to the opposition.[45]

On the issue of peace and war, he reiterated his peaceful intentions but said it was "an awful fallacy to suppose that you will have lasting peace and security if you do not command the esteem of the nations of the world by taking a self-respecting position which they know that any courageous and indomitable people could not fail to take. That is not the path to war." Hughes seemed to be saying that if the Wilson administration had stood up to the belligerents, whether England with its blacklist or Germany with its submarines, these countries would have backed down against the United States. Perhaps so, but in the atmosphere of 1916, the Republican candidate was sending unwelcome warning signals to voters fearful of an incident that might lead to war.

The Roosevelt problem for the Republicans continued. The Democrats had been directing their fire as much against him as they did toward Hughes. In Chicago on October 18, Secretary of the Treasury McAdoo noted Roosevelt's statement that he would have seized all the interned German ships after the *Lusitania* went down. "Mr. Roosevelt's actions would have resulted in war between the United States and Germany," argued McAdoo. The secretary also said that "if Mr. Hughes is made President, Mr. Roosevelt will be the dominating influence and will direct our foreign and domestic policies. Therefore, every explicit utterance of Mr. Roosevelt, and every implicit utterance of Mr. Hughes shows that if elected America will be forced into war with some nation." Accordingly, McAdoo concluded, "the rights and honor of the American people are safe in the hands of Woodrow Wilson and will be upheld unflinchingly in the face of the entire world."[46]

As for Roosevelt himself, he had during October been receiving letters that told him "the Hughes campaign is on the rocks" and that "The Republicans and Hughes should cease trying to be all things to all things." Roosevelt's journalist friend Cal O'Laughlin concluded on November 3 that Wilson was going to carry the Middle West because "Hughes has been beaten by himself. He has really been a critic, not a statesman." O'Laughlin was too pessimistic about the region's position, but his overall warning had merit.[47]

With the prospect of the election slipping away and the hated Wilson about to be returned, Roosevelt intensified his attacks on the president. Prominent Republicans asked him to speak at Cooper Union in New York City on November 3, and he responded with one of the most scathing diatribes any former president ever directed against an incumbent.[48] He compared Wilson to the pre–Civil War executive James Buchanan, revived the Valley Forge charges against Newton D. Baker, and alleged "that there is not a bandit leader in Mexico who does not know that if he can show enough strength he can at any moment make Mr. Wilson not merely turn back but humbly kiss his hand; kiss the hand that is red with the blood of our men, women, and children." Reporters who covered the address said that Roosevelt "time after time roused those of the crowd of 25,000 that were able to get into the hall to frenzied cheers."[49]

Turning to the war in Europe, Roosevelt said that Germany despised Wilson and the *Lusitania* was sunk in consequence. Playing on Wilson's summer residence at Shadow Lawn, Roosevelt, like a musician developing a theme, went on an extended riff that touched the boundaries of good taste. "There should be shadows enough at Shadow Lawn; the shadows of men, women, and children who have risen from the ooze of the ocean bottom and from graves in foreign lands; the shadow of the helpless whom Mr. Wilson did not dare protect lest he might have to face danger." Roosevelt concluded: "those are the shadows proper for Shadow Lawn; the shadows of deeds that were never done; the shadows of lofty words that were followed by no action; the shadows of the tortured dead."[50]

In its coverage of the speech, the *New-York Tribune* ran Roosevelt's remarks about Shadow Lawn in a box on the front page. Its account of the speech said it was "the Roosevelt of old—full of fire and with 'the punch' in every sentence—that time after time raised those in the crowd of 25,000 that were able to get into the hall to frenzied cheers." The New York *Sun*, another pro-Hughes paper said, "T.R. Riddles Wilson as Thousands Cheer," and later added, "Colonel Roosevelt put Shadow Lawn on the map by cataloguing the shadows. And what shadows."[51]

And yet what was Roosevelt saying but that the United States should be in the conflict on the Allied side? It may well have been what Hughes, like Root, Lodge, and Taft thought at the time, but it was not what large portions of the electorate wanted, as the Democrats emphasized. In their pre-election advertising, the Democrats ran a cartoon showing Hughes promising to name a strong cabinet. All the cabinet members depicted were Theodore Roosevelt, some with captions that said "peace is hell" and "I want war." The text of the ad said "Roosevelt says we should hang our heads in shame because we are not at *war* with Germany on behalf of Belgium." The choice, in the words of the ad, was "Wilson and Peace with Honor or Hughes with Roosevelt and War." Roosevelt's Cooper Union address, justly famous for his Shadow Lawn theme, was probably just the thing Hughes did not need as the election impended.[52]

During the first weekend in November as the election loomed on November 7, the likelihood of a positive verdict seemed clear to Hughes and other Republicans. So confident was he that Hughes decided not to reply to any of Wilson's final attacks. The election was in the bag. Said the *Sun*, "If Charles E. Hughes is defeated tomorrow he will be the most astonished man in the United States. No aspirant for the Presidency was ever more quietly confident of victory. So far as Mr. Hughes is concerned nothing remains except to tabulate his pluralities." His confidence stemmed from large, enthusiastic rallies and parades in New York City during those final days. The crowd at Madison Square Garden cheered him for more than a half an hour and as he stood at the rostrum "if ever a man showed the sense of confidence and pleasure Charles Evans Hughes was that man."[53]

The vigorous and legal wagering that went on at the curb market (a forerunner of the American Stock Exchange) and in the major hotels produced lavish betting on the outcome of the presidential contest. Newspapers tracked the wagering on a daily basis on the theory that this revealed information on voter sentiment. The two preeminent scholars of election bets estimate that bettors put down, in 2015 dollars, about $217 million. Newspapers reported that boxing promoter Tex Rickard and notorious gambler and underworld figure Arnold Rothstein were active in placing bets.[54] Odds stood at 10 to 8 for Hughes as Election Day neared.

The two parties flooded the nation's newspapers with full-page election advertising. The Republicans with their sizable war chest could out-spend the Democrats and did so in the final seven days. Colonel House recorded in his diary that Wilson "did not like the Republican expenditure of money to defeat him as evidenced by the full page advertisements in the morning papers. The Republicans had sixteen columns to our one and a half."[55] The full-page notices for Hughes touted the virtues of tariff protection, arguing that "the Democratic party is always the Party for worldwide Free Trade and European Prices in America." Under the heading "The Broken Promise," the Republicans charged that the Democrats were responsible for higher commodity prices and the rising cost of living. Finally, the Republicans sought to rebut the contention that the president had "kept us out of war," citing the continuing violence in Mexico and loss of life on the high seas.[56]

Because of the stakes in the election, high-profile newspaper and individual endorsements were more coveted and sought after in 1916. Intellectuals divided over the merits of Hughes and Wilson in print and in person. Hughes could claim the support of former progressives such as Raymond Robins who stumped for the Republican candidate against the Democrats. He urged Democrats and Republicans to rally behind Hughes as the more progressive choice in the race.[57] The president of Cornell, Jacob Gould Schurman, citing the Hughes record in New York, wrote that Hughes was the true reformer in the race as against Wilson who was in thrall to the antiquated ideas of the Democrats.[58] On the other side, the editors of *The New Republic*, a new reform journal started in 1914, changed their mind about Wilson's qualifications. Walter Lippmann, making "the Case for Wilson," concluded that "the weak, impractical doctrinaire has proved to be one of the great party leaders of American history."[59] The magazine's editor, Herbert Croly, informed a Republican friend, "the Democratic Congress under his leadership has accomplished a large amount of legislation of which I thoroughly approve and which really has constructive national significance."[60] Former attorney general and secretary of state Richard Olney wrote a long article in defense of Wilson and critical of Hughes that appeared in the New York *World* and attracted much attention.[61]

While Hughes bubbled with confidence in the last weeks, the president, though outwardly positive, was less certain about his chances of reelection. "I am told on good authority," wrote Nicholas Murray Butler, "that Wilson is now certain of his own reelection, although he did not have that feeling two weeks ago." Whatever his inner convictions, Wilson listened to a radical suggestion from Colonel House. If Hughes triumphed, Wilson would ask Robert Lansing to resign as secretary of state. Hughes would be named in his place. Wilson and Vice President Thomas Riley Marshall would in turn resign and Hughes, based on the line of succession then existing, would become president at once. The alternative would be a four-month interval before Hughes could take power. Wilson wrote a personal letter to Lansing on November 5 that said if the scheme went into effect "there would be no doubt in any quarter here how that [foreign] policy was to be directed, towards what objects and by what means. I would have no right to risk the peace of the nation by remaining in office after I had lost my authority."[62] The letter was put aside as the nation prepared to vote.

On that final weekend, the *New-York Tribune* told its readers that Hughes seemed certain of election though the reporters acknowledged that the race was close. The editors of the paper gave Hughes 252 certain electoral votes, including California and Kansas, with 42 electoral votes more probable for his column. They assigned Ohio as probable for Wilson. They expected Hughes to carry his home state of New York

Clifford Berryman captured the tense mood of the voters on November 7, 1916. Courtesy of the Library of Congress.

and he was likely to prevail also in New Jersey.[63] The final statement from Hughes said: "I believe that the American people have determined that the nation shall regain its international prestige and that the rights of American citizens shall be protected throughout the world."[64] The Republicans still felt confident that they would win the presidency, as they had believed for so long. However, for the first time in almost thirty years, since the close election of 1888, no one really knew how the election would turn out as the long campaign wound down to its conclusion.

8 THE ELECTION AND ITS MEANING

Election Day, November 7, finally came with a forecast of generally fair weather except for rain and snow in upper Minnesota and Michigan. The Weather Service expected moderate temperatures in most of the country. Though there had been complaints that "I have never seen a time when the general public was so indifferent to the outcome of a national election," the voters came out when it mattered.[1] The turnout of 59.7 percent in the northern states was up from 55.9 percent in 1912. In a more dramatic fashion, turnout was up over 18 percent in the four western states that had voted in previous contests. Despite the recurrent fears of apathy, the American people showed with their votes that they cared about the election and the issues that two major candidates had advanced.

The major New York newspapers competed to see which one could first call the final result for the readers gathered outside their buildings. That seemed an easy task after the polls closed in the eastern states. As the hand-counted returns came in during the early evening of November 7, matters seemed to be going exceedingly well for Hughes and the Republicans. The GOP was sweeping the Northeast and amassing a striking total of electoral votes. New York fell into the Hughes column by more than 120,000 votes as persistent Democratic factionalism crippled the party's campaign. Connecticut, Massachusetts, and New Jersey in clockwork succession also went for Hughes. Both the *New-York Tribune* and then the *New York Times* conceded the election to Hughes. The Democratic New York *World* fell into line with its own concession to Hughes. After all, the Republican candidate had almost 245 electoral votes and seemed certain to win when the western states were recorded. Ecstatic Republicans felt for a few brief hours that they had finally disposed of Woodrow Wilson.

By the early morning on November 8, however, the vote-counting situation had undergone a dramatic change. As returns flowed in from the West, it was clear that the president was running better than anyone had expected in that region. State after state went for Wilson, including the crucial 24 votes of Ohio and the dozen electoral votes of Kansas, a state that the Republicans had counted in their favor for weeks. The totals at dawn as the newspapers went to bed with their election coverage stood at 247 for Hughes and 251 for Wilson. In doubt were California with 13 electoral votes and Minnesota with 12. Over the next several days Minnesota fell to Hughes and California went Democratic to bolster Wilson's total. New Hampshire came into the Wilson column by a scant 56 votes. The close election hung in the balance.

By the time the election was decided, it was evident that Wilson had prevailed by a narrow margin in the electoral count. The president had 277 electoral votes to 254 for Hughes. In the popular vote the result was 9,129,000 for Wilson to 8,538,000 for Hughes. In several states the vote was very close. Wilson carried New Hampshire by those 56 ballots, North Dakota by 1,735, New Mexico by 2,530, and the decisive California by 3,773.

The Republicans and Hughes found the losing outcome stunning. It had all seemed to be going their way on Election Day in the early count. The *Chicago Tribune* had a story on November 8 that called Hughes the "probable winner," and the corporation lawyer William Nelson Cromwell wired Hughes on November 8: "I rejoice in the reestablishment of Republican principles and administration under your splendid leadership in the most serious period of our national life and send you warm personal congratulations and well wishes." For a day, the Republicans savored victory.[2] Surely the western states would not reject the Republicans.

Then as the tide turned early on the morning of November 8 and the count became more and more trending in Wilson's favor as the day progressed, the question became what were the Republicans going to do in the face of the apparent Wilson victory. What had seemed so certain a success on the evening of November 7 had been transformed into a stunning personal triumph for the president that so many in the Republican camp reviled and despised. On November 9, Chairman Willcox once again assured the press that Hughes would still win, while party operatives combed the state returns searching for the missing Republican votes they were sure were out there somewhere in the nation's mid-section. Reporters looked back to the contest in 1876 between Rutherford B. Hayes (R) and Samuel J. Tilden (D) where late returns pointed first to a deadlocked contest and, after months of negotiations, an eventual one-vote electoral vote victory for the Republican. Willcox issued a strong statement: "Any men who attempt to steal the Presidency from Charles Evans Hughes will do so at their peril." With the election returns running against his candidate, Willcox also hedged. "Anybody who intimates that Charles Evans Hughes would permit any man or group of men to attempt to steal the Presidency for him is a contemptible scoundrel and knows it."[3]

The predicament for the Republicans was whether they should institute proceedings for recounts in states that Wilson had won by only a narrow margin. The situation in Minnesota seemed to be moving toward Hughes, which would take his electoral vote total up to 255. By November 11 Hughes and the Republicans had decided to wait for confirmation of the official count in the contested states. Some Republicans wanted to push harder for recounts, but Hughes's view of the matter stood up. As the official counts arrived, it became unmistakably evident that Wilson had in fact won the states credited to him and the final count left the president with 277 electoral votes to 254 for Hughes. If California had gone to Hughes, he would have prevailed by three electoral votes. Waiting, as Hughes did for the official returns from California, meant that he did not actually concede defeat until a telegram to Wilson arrived on November 22. It gave Wilson a private chance to twit Hughes. The president told his brother that the concession telegram was "a little moth-eaten when it got here but quite legible."[4] Winners get to poke fun at losers, but Hughes, as the temporary leader of his party, had every right to play the game out to the end. Suppose the official returns revealed he had won. He conceded when he had to and acted in a responsible manner as a candidate.

The election also had an effect on the alignment of the two parties in Congress. The Democrats retained control of the upper house by an eleven-seat margin. The Republicans defeated Majority Leader John

Worth Kern in Indiana and picked up a second seat in that state. The GOP also added a senator from Maine. The Republican senators who served after 1917 approached the policies of the president with deep skepticism and distrust that would carry over into the struggle over the League of Nations in 1919.

Wilson turned out to have no coattails as far as the House of Representatives was concerned. The Republicans gained fourteen seats to draw even with the Democrats at 215 each. The Democrats persuaded members from minor parties to vote with them to organize the House. The thin majority of the president's party meant that members from the South exercised great influence on legislation. Their sectional behavior would give the Republicans after 1916 cause to accuse their rivals of a bias against northern voters. That charge would gain salience in 1917 and 1918.

When the election was decided, extensive post-mortems began. Wilson came in for ample credit as the first Democratic president since Andrew Jackson to be elected to two consecutive terms. He had succeeded despite everything the Republicans could throw at him in the way of money, innuendo, and party unity. The president increased his total vote count over 1912 by more than 2,830,000 ballots. The *New-York Tribune,* which had been very critical of Wilson, carried an editorial entitled "The Real Answer" that said "such personal satisfaction as can be drawn from the result belongs to Mr. Wilson. He is entitled to it." The president was, said the editors, "a man to be reckoned with politically because of his hold upon popular imagination and public approval."[5] The New York *World,* long the most prominent Wilson newspaper, called the result "the most substantial sort of indorsement from friends in every quarter whom he has made since he became President."[6]

His defeat left Charles Evans Hughes bewildered since he had been so certain of victory. In his autobiographical notes, he wrote, "I still should have been elected had it not been for the effectiveness, particularly in the middle west, of the Democratic slogan 'He kept us out of war.'"

At no time did Hughes recognize and admit his own failings as a candidate, the initial failure of the acceptance speech, his personal choice, with the advice of Mrs. Hughes, of William Willcox as his chairman, and his inability to change his campaign style in the face of frequent suggestions to do so from Republicans in his entourage.[7]

Among Republicans Wilson's victory went down hard and there was no sign of an abatement in partisan contention. They had hoped so much that Hughes would prevail and restore order to a political world that seemed to them out of joint. "I feel the re-election of President Wilson is a national calamity," said one worker at the Republican National Committee.[8] "The election was a bitter disappointment to me," wrote William Howard Taft, who had seen the Republican defeat coming. "Roosevelt contributed to our defeat as much as any other cause," he added.[9] For his part, Roosevelt wrote William Willcox, "Outside of Hughes and his immediate circle of friends, I question if there was a man more keenly disappointed than I was."[10] Henry Cabot Lodge wrote Hughes to say "how deeply distressed and grieved I am by the result of the election." He blamed "life-long, rock ribbed Republicans chiefly of the country towns, and in the Northwest"—the Scandinavian farmers affected by the peace issue.[11]

Much attention focused on the decisive role of California in the final outcome. When happy Democrats wanted to have a banquet to celebrate the state's role in Wilson's victory, the president told visitors, "I owe no special thanks to California for casting its vote for me and certainly no gratitude is due to any person or any state for performing a duty. California but did her duty and I am not inclined to engage in fulsome expressions of gratitude." Wilson's lack of political sensitivity on such matters contributed to the problems he faced with politicians during his second term.[12]

Some of the election assessments focused on Hughes and his failure to do what his enthusiastic backers had forecast before his nomination. A savvy reporter had concluded even before the election occurred that "frankly as a candidate who was expected to rally the boys, he was a frost." Charles W. Eliot of Harvard told a British friend that Hughes was "a huge disappointment to his party managers." Moreover "He was provided with no serious issue by his party, and invented none himself."[13] The Republicans had now selected three smart individuals in a row—Roosevelt, Taft, and Hughes—as their presidential candidates and in 1920 the governor of Kansas said, "We have had all the superman business the party is likely to want."[14]

An acerbic evaluation of the Hughes candidacy came from Warren G. Harding, who had watched Wilson and the Democrats carry Ohio, a state that the Republicans believed should be theirs in every national election. After the GOP lost Ohio by more than 89,000 ballots, Harding moaned: "The general impression is very general here, as well as in Ohio, that he would have fared much better had he gone to his summer residence after the speech of notification and acceptance and remained there and retained the halo about his head which came on his exceptional nomination."[15]

Hughes never acknowledged any failings as a candidate. He laid all the blame off on Wilson's peace theme, which he clearly regarded as dishonest. His refusal to accept advice about the weaknesses of his campaign style reflected his life-long belief in his own superior mental abilities in public life. Would he have been a more successful president than Wilson in handling the challenges of World War I? It is easy to think so when viewing the political debacle of Wilson's second term. But Hughes would also have confronted the societal and logistical demands that crippled the American war effort.

Roosevelt soon informed friends that the Republicans had erred in not identifying the party with his anti-Wilson, pro-war posture and campaigning accordingly with himself at the top of the ticket. "Their one chance of winning was with me" and "it would have been to their enormous advantage to have nominated me."[16] Against that were comments such as those included in a mocking telegram sent to Roosevelt from "New York Democrats" saying "Wilson ought to give you a cabinet position as you elected him beyond any doubt."[17] Many people wrote to Roosevelt to tell him that he could have won as the Republican nominee. Roosevelt as a candidate would not have been open to the charge of equivocation that dogged Hughes, but his pro-war and anti–German American language would likely have produced the defections that Henry Cabot Lodge described in even greater abundance. As Charles Eliot noted, "his unmannerly efforts, however, in all probability increased considerably the number of votes cast for Wilson."[18] Roosevelt would likely have lost Minnesota, for example, and could well have been in trouble in Indiana. It may have been personally consoling to Roosevelt to think that he would have won a straight-up battle with Wilson, but it would have been more likely that the president would have beaten him rather easily.

Following the defeat, Roosevelt seemed at once the likely choice of the Republicans in 1920, but whether he would have been selected had he lived, is one of the great historical "what ifs." In 1916 he had gone his own way as a surrogate and, with his abundant self-confidence, had not coordinated what he was saying with the case that Hughes was making. As ever Roosevelt chafed in a subordinate role. It might have been difficult, however, for the GOP to swallow Roosevelt after he had, for many party members, cost the GOP two national elections.

Beyond the praise or blame attached to the various candidates and their supporters, there was agreement that the election revealed striking differences between the eastern and western states in their political attitudes. "The scepter of power is passing to the West in conjunction with the South and Southwest. Mr. Wilson has shown us all that we must roll up our political maps and make one entirely new." The sectional coalition that William Jennings Bryan had sought to assemble in 1896 now seemed to have been established by the president against Hughes and the Republicans.[19]

While they pondered the sectional implications of Wilson's success, commentators identified the president's ability to win the votes of labor, farmers, and women as the elements in the victorious coalition. The Adamson Act and the enactment of the eight-hour day for railroad men proved a powerful attraction for working-class voters, as the Republicans recognized too late in the campaign. By highlighting his opposition to the law, and calling the measure a wages bill, Hughes may have unwittingly stressed that Wilson was for labor in general, which helped him with all workers.

Farmers in the plains states added their clout to Wilson. The president's "greatest strength was in the great agricultural counties known as the Kansas wheat belt," wrote the Topeka *Capital*, noting the high prices for farm goods in those areas. One unhappy Republican said, "There was a fat rich cushion of prosperity and the farmer was lulled upon it, he refused to think." It all added up to the "fatty degeneration of the Kansas spirit."[20] Farmers, of course, noted all the measures that Wilson endorsed and Congress passed aimed at their profession—the Farm Loan bank, the rural credits law, and other measures.

The women's vote, on which Hughes had counted so much at the start of his campaign with his support of the suffrage amendment, seemed in the end to have gone for Wilson, largely on the peace issue. There were twelve states where women could vote and Hughes carried only two, Illinois and Oregon. Wilson won the other ten, especially California, which proved decisive. The National Woman's Party, which made so much noise for Hughes, did not deliver for the Republicans as they had promised. The train of the Hughesettes aroused as much irritation as support for the Republican with their well-covered campaign train.

Some observers contended that the result would have been the same if women had not voted at all.[21]

Historians have seen in the 1916 election a foreshadowing of the New Deal coalition of Franklin D. Roosevelt. The elements that would exist in the 1930s were there in 1916—the South, labor, farmers, and liberals. Only African Americans were absent, put off by the segregationist racial policies of the administration. The Wilson forces used class consciousness to structure their appeal to the voters, along with reliance on the peace issue.

The defection of Irish and Catholic voters, which had so worried Democratic strategists throughout the year, failed to materialize in the crushing manner that had been forecast. Despite their animus against Great Britain and its policies, including the execution of Roger Casement, Irish Americans responded to the existence of peace and prosperity and voted in their customary manner. Catholics followed suit, even in the face of the disapproval of the hierarchy toward the president.

Analysis of the election soon broke down into discussions of what had happened in the close states. Because it seemed to tip the scales between Hughes and Wilson, California came in for the most retrospective attention. The alleged "snub" of Hiram Johnson became the easy explanation, which subsequent writers have debunked. Among Republicans Johnson added party disloyalty to his radical reputation and ended his future presidential hopes even after his election to the Senate in 1916 over the father of future American war hero, George S. Patton, Jr.

Though it was the only Midwestern state that Wilson carried, Ohio did not loom as large, despite being a crucial part of Wilson's electoral vote total. Without Ohio, California would never have mattered. Republicans believed that the eight-hour day was the deciding element in their state along with the peace issue toward Europe and Mexico. The issue of prohibition, which was emerging as a force in state politics, also cut against the GOP. "Wets" voted the straight Democratic ticket to be sure that the Republican governor, a friend of prohibition, went down. Myron Herrick's losing Senate race against Democrat Atlee Pomerene also aided Wilson. The big result of this contest, other than Wilson's win, was to help make Warren G. Harding more of a national player.[22]

Right after the voting in 1916, predictions of a permanent shift in electoral alignments were prevalent. Of course it never happened. Soon after he knew he was reelected, Wilson launched an ill-fated peace initiative that did not work because of the intransigence of both the Allies and the Central Powers. Then Germany in late January 1917 embarked on unrestricted submarine warfare that brought American entry into the war by early April 1917. Though Wilson knew that war could come at any time because of decisions that the warring powers made, the slogan of "he kept us out of war" sounded hollow a scant six months after the election.

In the months of belligerency that followed, President Wilson and Congress under the Democrats followed policies that demolished the fragile electoral coalition that the Democrats had so painstakingly assembled in 1916. Part of the problem lay in the very nature of the Democratic Party. Southern lawmakers came from the bloc of states where the Republicans had little or no presence because of race. These politicians enacted legislation that promoted their regional interests. As a result, the issue of sectionalism, which Hughes had mentioned in vain in the 1916 campaign, returned to great salience two years later.

The Lever Act of 1917 gave the president the authority to fix prices on important agricultural products as part of the war effort. Farmers in the grain states of the Middle West disliked controls, which held down their profits, especially when the president set the price of wheat well below the existing market price. Southern cotton farmers faced no such limits because of their clout with members of Congress from their region. The sympathy of Wilson and his administration, so great in November 1916, eroded as the price policy continued.

Labor unrest marked the wartime years as unions sought wage gains. The administration created a National War Labor Board that made some concessions to unions, but strikes and lockouts continued with a lessening of support for Democrats among those workers who had supported Wilson in 1916. Chronic labor struggles persisted into the postwar period.

The White House also alienated progressives by supporting the repressive policies of both the Postmaster General and the Justice Department. Albert S. Burleson and the Post Office banned publications from radicals who opposed the war. The assaults on Socialists and radicals from the government drew no criticism from the president, who now seemed obsessed with fighting the war. A liberal commentator summed up the abuse of civil liberties to Colonel House: "The method now being pursued is breaking down liberal support of the war and is tending to divide the country's articulate opinion into fanatical jingoism and fanatical patriotism."[23]

Wilson had given rhetorical support to woman suffrage in 1916. A year later protestors outside the White House were jailed when they criticized the president for being slow on the issue. Democrats from the South, fearing that suffrage for women could lead to black voting, blocked suffrage in Congress. The apparent reluctance of the president and his party to act added to discontent with his leadership. Meanwhile the prohibition issue, gaining in salience, split wets from drys among Democrats and increased the internal tensions of the party.

The Republicans, on the other hand, still driven by their bitter hatred of Wilson, found a new leader in Will H. Hays, a young Indiana politician, who was elected as chair of the Republican National Committee in early 1918. Hays played down the party splits of the past and stressed unity. A former Progressive, Harold Ickes, wrote that "the Republican national Committee has infused new blood into its party organization by the selection of a young, vigorous man as its chairman."[24] By his emphasis on how the Republicans were contributing to the war effort, Hays found a way for Republicans to work together while indicting the administration for ineptitude and blunders in mobilizing the country. As Hays put it in 1918, "Every Republican vote cast is another nail in the Kaiser's coffin, every Republican Congressman is another stone piled on his tomb."[25]

Wilson, whose whole career had been marked by political good fortune, now seemed to have forfeited his ability to remain in touch with the currents of public opinion. He made few speeches and abandoned press conferences. He seemed a remote distant figure, confined to the White House, without the contact with the average citizen that had been established during his first term. In the process Democratic fortunes suffered in the face of resurgent Republicans.

Whatever gains the Democrats might have established with their victory in 1916 were extinguished in the 1918 elections in which the Republicans came roaring back into control of both Houses of Congress. Wilson asked the American people to endorse his leadership and elect Democrats in a famous appeal on October 25, 1918. The Republicans labeled this political gesture an attack on their patriotism. With William Howard Taft and Theodore Roosevelt now reunited and a semblance of their earlier friendship restored against their common enemy in the president and his record, their partnership keynoted a Republican sweep in the House and a narrow GOP control of the Senate.

The end of the war came shortly after the election results. For President Wilson there was no political solace in the Republican victory. He added to the accumulated ills of the Democrats when he resolved to use American success as a springboard to establish a League of Nations at the peace conference in Paris that began in early 1919. The Republicans in the Senate, led by Wilson's implacable foe, Henry Cabot Lodge, made it clear that they would not endorse any treaty containing the league without substantial changes in its text. The president secured some alteration to appease his critics, and returned with a pact containing the league in the summer of 1919.

Faced with continuing Republican opposition to the league, Wilson went on a nationwide speaking tour in September. His orations swayed few votes in the upper house, and then Wilson's health broke. He became a stroke victim after his return to Washington, and was an invalid for the rest of his presidency. Leaderless, the Democrats drifted while the country experienced inflation, labor strife, a hunt for subversive radicals, sectional discord, and a repudiation of the Democrats. Wilson dreamed of a third term and vindication, but it was not to be.

The Democrats selected a former governor of Ohio, James M. Cox, to face another resident of the state, Warren G. Harding, in a presidential election in which the Republicans had everything working in their favor. The Democrats never had a chance to win. The closeness of 1916 was a distant memory in the autumn of 1920 as the Republicans rolled to a landslide victory for Harding and his running mate, Calvin Coolidge. Wilson left office on March 4, 1921, a broken man whose popularity had vanished since the euphoria of November 1916. He lived on in illness and seclusion until his death in February 1924.

Charles Evans Hughes had returned to private law practice by that time, but came back into public life to serve as one of Harding's "best minds" as secretary of state. He remained in office from 1921 to 1925, when he returned to private practice. Following the death of Chief Justice William Howard Taft in 1930, Herbert Hoover nominated Hughes to replace him. As chief justice Hughes served throughout the 1930s and was successful in defeating the so-called court-packing plan of Franklin D. Roosevelt in 1937. Hughes retired in 1941 and died in 1948. By that time his defeat at the hands of Wilson in 1916 seemed only an unfortunate episode in a distinguished legal and judicial career.

Because of American involvement in World War I and the subsequent defeat of the Democrats in 1920, followed by twelve years of Republican electoral dominance, the election of 1916 came to be seen as kind of a fluke resulting from the special circumstances of the period of American neutrality. The inherent Republican majority reappeared as it had since the 1890s, but Hughes lacked the talent to win the victory that ought to have been his.

The Republicans, still feeling the aftereffects of their 1912 debacle, turned to Hughes, who proved to be a much weaker candidate than he had seemed during the spring of 1916. Wilson, for his part, showed himself to be a much more opportunistic operator who capitalized on the weaknesses of his opponent throughout the contest. Despite the ample campaign funds at their disposal, the Republicans never found a winning formula.

In terms of performance in conducting the campaign, the two parties shifted roles in 1916. Where they had once been noted for the efficiency with which they conducted a presidential canvass, the Republicans under William Willcox never found their stride and stumbled all during the fall. The Democrats, in contrast, put aside their customary in-fighting behind Vance McCormick and made the most of their opportunities to win votes. It would be twenty years before the Democrats showed similar proficiency with the electorate behind Franklin D. Roosevelt.

As historians have noted, the 1916 election, even more than 1912, saw the two parties move toward ideological positions that would characterize their conflict for the remainder of the century. Especially after the adoption of the Adamson Act in September, the Republicans intensified their denunciations of class warfare and government interference in the economy. The GOP denounced Wilson's programs to assist individual elements in the nation and advanced arguments that the government should keep its hands out of the conduct of economic affairs. At the same time, the Democrats were saying that the government should do more rather than less to assist groups—such as farmers, laborers, and small business—who were in need.

What the election did not do was to shake the Republican conviction that they were the natural governing party and were entitled to lead against the disloyal and feckless Democrats. Wilson had not gotten 50 percent of the popular vote, which buttressed the continuing Republican assumption that he was a minority president and therefore lacked legitimacy. In fact, because they regarded Wilson as a lucky accident, the Republicans felt even more justified in confronting the administration with all-out opposition. It was no more than the Democrats deserved for how they had behaved during 1913–1916.

Soon after the election Wilson was arguing that the country should put the rancor of the election aside and get about working together. "I am glad that the political campaign is over and that we can settle down in soberness and unity of spirit to work for the welfare of the country, without thinking of the advantage of parties."[26] What he did not understand was that no such period of partisan reconciliation was possible for the Republicans as long as the GOP was out of power. Wilson was a usurper who had to be stopped. In that sense the president and the Democrats assumed that the voters had given them legitimacy and the right to wield power. They could not have been more mistaken. Without even a pause to let the Democrats savor their victory, the Republicans resumed their posture of unyielding opposition to the Wilson administration. Wilson had won the election, but the legitimacy he also craved was denied to him. So the election of 1916 had only settled which man was going to occupy the White House and hold power until March 4, 1921. For the unhappy Republicans that was a bitter outcome to absorb. During the war Wilson would say "politics is adjourned" until the fighting ended. He never realized that for his enemies politics would never stop until Woodrow Wilson left his office in disgrace. That was the continuing impact of the election of 1916.

APPENDIX A
VOTES CAST IN REPUBLICAN PRIMARIES, 1916

State	Hughes	Cummins	Ford	Roosevelt	Favorite Sons	Unpledged	Scattered
California						236,277	
Illinois				15,348	155,945		1,689
Indiana						176,078	
Iowa		40,257					
Maryland*							
Massachusetts				45,117		60,462	
Michigan			83,057		92,237		
Minnesota		54,214					16,403
Montana		10,415					1,173
Nebraska	15,837	29,850	26,684	2,256			13,780
New Hampshire						9,687	
New Jersey	383			1,076			
New York						147,038	
North Dakota							33,225
Ohio	469		1,683	1,932	122,165		14,428
Oregon	56,764	27,558					10,593
Pennsylvania	1,804		20,265	12,359	233,095		2,682
South Dakota		29,656					
Vermont	5,480			1,931			423
Wisconsin					110,052		1,347

* No primary held.

Source: Louise Overacker, *The Presidential Primary* (New York: Macmillan, 1924), 237.

APPENDIX B

ELECTORAL VOTES, 1916

State	Democratic Woodrow Wilson	Republican Charles E. Hughes	Electoral Votes for Wilson	Electoral Votes for Hughes
Alabama	99,409	28,662	12	
Arizona	33,170	20,524	3	
Arkansas	112,211	48,879	9	
California	466,829	462,516	13	
Colorado	178,816	102,308	6	
Connecticut	99,786	106,514		7
Delaware	24,573	26,011		3
Florida	55,984	14,611	6	
Georgia	127,754	11,294	14	
Idaho	70,054	55,638	4	
Illinois	950,229	1,152,549		29
Indiana	334,063	341,045		15
Iowa	218,699	280,349		13
Kansas	314,588	277,658	10	
Kentucky	269,990	241,854	13	
Louisiana	79,875	6,466	10	
Maine	64,033	69,508		6
Maryland	138,359	117,347	8	
Massachusetts	247,885	268,784		18
Michigan	286,775	339,097		15
Minnesota	179,152	179,544		12
Mississippi	80,422	4,253	10	
Missouri	398,032	369,339	18	
Montana	101,063	66,750	4	
Nebraska	158,227	117,771	8	
Nevada	17,776	12,127	3	
New Hampshire	43,781	43,725	4	
New Jersey	211,018	268,982		14
New Mexico	33,527	31,152	3	
New York	759,426	879,238		45
North Carolina	168, 383	120,890	12	
North Dakota	55,206	53,471	5	
Ohio	604,161	514,753	24	
Oklahoma	148,113	97,233	10	

(continued on next page)

State	Democratic Woodrow Wilson	Republican Charles E. Hughes	Electoral Votes for Wilson	Electoral Votes for Hughes
Oregon	120,087	126,813		5
Pennsylvania	521,784	703,823		38
Rhode Island	40,394	44,858		5
South Carolina	61,846	1,550	9	
South Dakota	59,191	64,217		5
Tennessee	153,280	116,223	12	
Texas	286,514	64,999	20	
Utah	84,145	54,137	4	
Vermont	22,708	40,250		4
Washington	183,388	167,208	7	
West Virginia	140,403	143,123		7
Wisconsin	191,363	220,822		13
Wyoming	28,316	21,698	3	
TOTAL	9,126,868	8,548,728	277	254

Source: David Leip, *Dave Leip's Atlas of U.S. Presidential Elections*, http//www.uselectionatlas.org/.

APPENDIX C

WOODROW WILSON'S SECOND INAUGURAL ADDRESS, MARCH 4, 1917

My fellow citizens: The four years which have elapsed since last I stood in this place have been crowded with counsel and action of the most vital interest and consequence. Perhaps no equal period in our history has been so fruitful of important reforms in our economic and industrial life or so full of significant changes in the spirit and purpose of our political action. We have sought very thoughtfully to set our house in order, to correct the grosser errors and abuses of our industrial life, liberate and quicken the processes of our national genius and energy, and lift our politics to a broader view of the people's essential interests. It is a record of singular variety and singular distinction. But I shall not attempt to review it. It speaks for itself and will be of increasing influence as the years go by. This is not the time for retrospect. It is the time, rather, to speak our thoughts and purposes concerning the present and the immediate future.

Although we have centered counsel and action with such unusual concentration and success upon the great problems of domestic legislation to which we addressed ourselves four years ago, other matters have more and more forced themselves upon our attention, matters lying outside our own life as a nation and over which we had no control, but which, despite our wish to remain free of them, have drawn us more and more irresistibly into their own current and influence.

It has been impossible to avoid them. They have affected the life of the whole world. They have shaken men everywhere with a passion and an apprehension they never knew before. It has been hard to preserve calm counsel while the thought of our own people swayed this way and that under their influence. We are a composite and cosmopolitan people. We are of the blood of all the nations that are at war. The currents of our thoughts as well as the currents of our trade run quick at all seasons back and forth between us and them. The war inevitably set its mark from the first alike upon our minds, our industries, our commerce, our politics, and our social action. To be indifferent to it or independent of it was out of the question.

And yet all the while we have been conscious that we were not part of it. In that consciousness, despite many divisions, we have drawn closer together. We have been deeply wronged upon the seas, but we have not wished to wrong or injure in return; have retained throughout the consciousness of standing in some sort apart, intent upon an interest that transcended the immediate issues of the war itself. As some of the injuries done us have become intolerable we have still been clear that we wished nothing for ourselves that we were not ready to demand for all mankind, fair dealing, justice, the freedom to live and be at ease against organized wrong.

It is in this spirit and with this thought that we have grown more and more aware, more and more certain that the part we wished to play was the part of those who mean to vindicate and fortify peace. We have been obliged to arm ourselves to make good our claim to a certain minimum of right and of freedom of action. We stand firm in armed neutrality since it seems that in no other way can we demonstrate what it is we insist upon and cannot forego. We may even be drawn on, by circumstances, not by our own purpose or desire, to a more active assertion of our rights as we see them and a more immediate association with the great struggle itself. But nothing will alter our thought or our purpose. They are too clear to be obscured. They are too deeply rooted in the principles of our national life to be altered. We desire neither conquest nor advantage. We wish nothing that can be had only at the cost of another people. We have always professed unselfish purpose and we covet the opportunity to prove that our professions are sincere.

There are many things still to do at home, to clarify our own politics and give new vitality to the industrial processes of our own life, and we shall do them as time and opportunity serve; but we realize that the greatest things that remain to be done must be done with the whole world for stage and in cooperation with the wide and universal forces of mankind, and we are making our spirits ready for those things. They will follow in the immediate wake of the war itself and will set civilization up again. We are provincials no longer. The tragical events of the thirty months of vital turmoil through which we have just passed have made us citizens of the world. There can be no turning back. Our fortunes as a nation are involved, whether we would have it so or not.

And yet we are not the less Americans on that account. We shall be more American if we but remain true to the principles in which we have been bred. They are not the principles of a province or of a single continent. We have known and boasted all along that they were the principles of a liberated mankind. These, therefore, are the things we shall stand for, whether in war or in peace:

That all nations are equally interested in the peace of the world and in the political stability of free peoples, and equally responsible for their maintenance;

That the essential principle of peace is the actual equality of nations in all matters of right or privilege;

That peace cannot securely or justly rest upon an armed balance of power;

That governments derive their just powers from the consent of the governed and that no other powers should be supported by the common thought, purpose, or power of the family of nations;

That the seas should be equally free and safe for the use of all peoples, under rules set up by common agreement and consent and that, so far as practicable, they should be accessible to all upon equal terms;

That national armaments should be limited to the necessities of national order and domestic safety;

That the community of interest and of power upon which peace must henceforth depend imposes upon each nation the duty of seeing to it that all influences proceeding from its own citizens meant to encourage or assist revolution in other states should be sternly and effectually suppressed and prevented.

I need not argue these principles to you, my fellow countrymen, they are your own, part and parcel of your own thinking and your own motive in affairs. They spring up native amongst us. Upon this as a platform of purpose and action we can stand together.

And it is imperative that we should stand together. We are being forged into a new unity amidst the fires that now blaze throughout the world. In their ardent heat we shall, in God's providence, let us hope, be purged of faction and division, purified of the errant humors of party and of private interest, and shall stand forth in the days to come with a new dignity of national pride and spirit. Let each man see to it that the dedication is in his own heart, the high purpose of the Nation in his own mind, ruler of his own will and desire.

I stand here and have taken the high and solemn oath to which you have been audience because the people of the United States have chosen me for this august delegation of power and have by their gracious judgment named their leader in affairs. I know now what the task means. I realize to the full the responsibility which it involves. I pray God I may be given the wisdom and the prudence to do my duty in the true spirit of this great people. I am their servant and can succeed only as they sustain and guide me by their confidence and counsel. The thing I shall count upon, the thing without which neither counsel nor action will avail, is the unity of America—an America united in feeling, in purpose, and in its vision of duty, of opportunity, and of service. We are to beware of all men who would turn the tasks and the necessities of the Nation to their own private profit or use them for the building up of private power; beware that no faction or disloyal intrigue break the harmony or embarrass the spirit of our people; beware that our government be kept pure and incorrupt in all its parts. United alike in the conception of our duty and in the high resolve to perform it in the face of all men, let us dedicate ourselves to the great task to which we must now set our hand. For myself I beg your tolerance, your countenance, and your united aid. The shadows that now lie dark upon our path will soon be dispelled and we shall walk with the light all about us if we be but true to ourselves,—to ourselves as we have wished to be known in the counsels of the world and in the thought of all those who love liberty and justice and the right exalted.

Source: "The Second Inaugural Address," in Arthur S. Link et al., eds., *The Papers of Woodrow Wilson, Volume 41: January 24–April 6, 1917* (Princeton, N.J.: Princeton University Press, 1983), 332–335.

NOTES

PREFACE

1 Heather Cox Richardson, *To Make Men Free: A History of the Republican Party* (New York: Basic Books, 2014), 176. I devoted more attention to the 1916 election in *The Republicans: A History of the Grand Old Party* (New York: Oxford University Press, 2014), 147–152.

2 S. D. Lovell, *The Presidential Election of 1916* (Carbondale: University of Southern Illinois Press, 1980). David Sarasohn, *The Party of Reform: Democrats in the Progressive Era* (Jackson and London: University of Mississippi Press, 1989). Meyer Nathan, "The Presidential Election of 1916 in the Middle West" (PhD diss., Princeton University, 1966), is a helpful study.

CHAPTER ONE. THE LEGACY OF 1912

1 Theodore Roosevelt to Benjamin Lindsey, November 16, 1912, in Elting E. Morison et al., eds., *The Letters of Theodore Roosevelt*, 8 vols. (Cambridge, Mass.: Harvard University Press, 1951–1954), 7: 650.

2 Joseph G. Cannon to Mabel Boardman, November 18, 1912, Box 6, Mabel Boardman Papers, Library of Congress.

3 Winthrop Murray Crane to William Howard Taft, November 12, 1912, Charles D. Hilles Papers, Sterling Memorial Library, Yale University, quoting a conservative Republican.

4 "Barnes against Compromise," *New York Times*, December 10, 1912; Cannon is quoted in "Leaders Approve Mr. Munsey's Plan to Unite Parties," *Washington Times*, January 9, 1913.

5 William Howard Taft to Julius Forstmann, April 18, 1913, William Howard Taft Papers, Library of Congress.

6 Frank A. Munsey, "A Possible Scheme for Amalgamating the Republican and Progressive Parties That Ought to Be Acceptable to Each," *Washington Times*, January 8, 1913.

7 "Roosevelt Frowns on Munsey Plan," *New York Times*, January 10, 1913; Roosevelt to Lemuel Quigg, May 20, 1913, Theodore Roosevelt Papers, Library of Congress (last quotation).

8 "The Massachusetts Warning," *New-York Tribune*, April 17, 1913. The *Tribune* did not favor that approach.

9 "South Loses Delegates in G.O.P. Convention," Washington, *Evening Star*, October 26, 1914.

10 "Wilson Appears before Congress; Asks Recognition as 'Human Being,'" *New-York Tribune*, April 9, 1913.

11 "President Wilson, the Democratic Party and the New 'Competitive Tariff,'" *Independent* 76 (October 9, 1913): 62.

12 Theodore E. Burton to Taft, July 30, 1913, Taft Papers.
13 Gus Karger to Taft, August 2, 1913, Taft Papers.
14 Joseph L. Bristow to Arthur Capper, September 18, 1913, Joseph L. Bristow Papers, Kansas State Historical Society, Topeka.
15 William P. Dillingham to James T. Williams, Jr., August 11, 1913, James T. Williams, Jr. Papers, Duke University Library.
16 Taft to James T. Williams, Jr., August 2, 1913, James T. Williams, Jr. Papers, Duke University Library.
17 Arthur S. Link, *Wilson: The New Freedom* (Princeton, N.J.: Princeton University Press, 1956), 264–267.
18 Link, *The New Freedom*, 268.
19 William Howard Taft to Mabel Boardman, April 22, 1913, Taft Papers.
20 Taft to Mrs. Eugene Stafford, July 7, 1914, Taft Papers. Taft gives his views on policy in the islands.
21 Malcolm Jennings to Warren G. Harding, September 15, 1914, Warren G. Harding Papers, Ohio Historical Society, Columbus, Ohio.
22 Bristow to J. R. Harrison, October 12, 1914, Bristow Papers; Lodge to Roosevelt, March 1, 1915, Roosevelt Papers.
23 Roosevelt to Arthur Lee, September 2, 1913, Papers of Lord Lee of Fareham, Courtauld Institute, London.
24 Harold Ickes to Amos Pinchot, December 2, 1912, Harold Ickes Papers, Box 37, Manuscript Division, Library of Congress.
25 Ibid.
26 Theodore Roosevelt to Arthur Lee, September 24, 1913, Papers of Lord Lee of Fareham.
27 Frank A. Munsey to Albert J. Beveridge, February 3, 1913, in Claude G. Bowers, *Beveridge and the Progressive Era* (Boston: Houghton Mifflin, 1932), 441–442.
28 Ickes to Amos Pinchot, December 2, 1912, Ickes Papers.
29 John A. Garraty, *Right-Hand Man: The Life of George W. Perkins* (New York: Harper & Brothers, 1957, 1960), 286.
30 Roosevelt to William Rockhill Nelson, July 1, 1913, Roosevelt Papers.
31 Donald Richberg to Harold Ickes, July 7, 1913, Ickes Papers.
32 Ashmun Brown to Erastus Brainerd, May 28, 1914, Erastus Brainerd Papers, University of Washington Library, Seattle.
33 Taft to Frank Brandegee, November 9, 1913, Taft Papers.
34 Herbert F. Margulies, *Reconciliation and Revival: James R. Mann and the House Republicans in the Wilson Era* (Westport, Conn.: Greenwood Press, 1996), 93, quotes Mann.
35 Gus Karger to Taft, January 9, 1914, Taft Papers.
36 "Clark Sees Business Boom," *Washington Post*, December 28, 1913.
37 Link, *The New Freedom*, 447.
38 "Republican Wins Jersey Congress Fight," *Washington Post*, April 8, 1914.
39 "Next House Won," *Washington Post*, April 9, 1914.
40 Margulies, *Reconciliation and Revival*, 94–95.

41 Louis A. Coolidge to James T. Williams, Jr., May 5, 1914, Williams, Jr. Papers.
42 Margulies, *Reconciliation and Revival,* 98, 103.
43 Ibid., 102–103.
44 Robert H. Watkins, "Democrats, in Fear of Losing House, and Holding Senate by Slender Vote, Place Blame on the Administration," *Washington Post,* June 28, 1914.
45 *Washington Times,* June 28, 1914.

CHAPTER TWO. THE 1914 ELECTION, THE GREAT WAR, AND BEYOND

1 John Milton Cooper, Jr., *Woodrow Wilson: A Biography* (New York: Alfred A. Knopf, 2009), 263.
2 Gus Karger to William Howard Taft, September 8, 1914, William Howard Taft Papers, Manuscript Division, Library of Congress.
3 "Declines to Help Party," *Washington Herald,* September 7, 1914.
4 Woodrow Wilson to Oscar W. Underwood, October 17, 1914, in Arthur S. Link et al., eds., *The Papers of Woodrow Wilson, Volume 32: September 6–December 31, 1914* (Princeton, N.J.: Princeton University Press, 1979), 174.
5 "Democratic Textbook Out," *New York Times,* September 22, 1914.
6 "Cabinet on the Stump," *Washington Post,* October 3, 1914.
7 "Democracy's Case before the Voters," *Literary Digest* 69 (October 31, 1914): 831.
8 "Clark Calls Wilson Great Peacemaker," *New York Times,* October 11, 1914; Lewis L. Gould, *Reform and Regulation: American Politics from Roosevelt to Wilson* (Prospect Heights, IL: Waveland Press, 1996), 176.
9 Philip C. Jessup, *Elihu Root,* 2 vols. (New York: Dodd, Mead, 1938), 2: 313.
10 Lodge to Roosevelt, March 1, 1915, Theodore Roosevelt Papers, Library of Congress.
11 "Penrose Closes Successful Tour," *Harrisburg Telegraph,* May 9, 1914.
12 "'Smash Penrose,' Roosevelt Urges Many Thousands," Philadelphia, *Evening Ledger,* October 27, 1914 (both quotations).
13 Pinchot to G. R. Robinson, December 29, 1914, author's collection.
14 Roosevelt to Hiram Johnson, November 6, 1914, Roosevelt Papers.
15 Roosevelt to Royal W. France, July 25, 1914, Roosevelt Papers.
16 Roosevelt to Hiram Johnson, July 16, 1914, Roosevelt Papers; George W. Wickersham to James T. Williams, Jr., July 31, 1914, James T. Williams, Jr. Papers, Duke University Library.
17 Roosevelt to William Allen White, September 2, 1914, William Allen White Papers, Manuscript Division, Library of Congress.
18 Cleveland H. Dodge to Wilson, November 5, 1914, in Arthur S. Link, ed., *The Papers of Woodrow Wilson, Volume 31*: 267.
19 Roosevelt to Hiram Johnson, November 6, 1914, Roosevelt Papers.
20 "Start House Fight on the War Tax Bill," *New York Times,* September 25, 1914.
21 "War Tax Big Issue," *Washington Post,* October 20, 1914.

22 Keokuk, Iowa, *Daily Gate City*, August 3, 1914.
23 Elihu Root to William Howard Taft, September 14, 1914, Taft Papers.
24 *Washington Post*, October 26, 1914.
25 "Hilles Says Tariff Is Issue for 1916," *New York Times*, December 21, 1914.
26 Theodore Roosevelt to William Allen White, November 7, 1914, Roosevelt Papers.
27 Ibid.
28 Roosevelt to Cecil Spring Rice, November 11, 1914, Roosevelt Papers.
29 Arthur S. Link, *Wilson: The New Freedom* (Princeton, N.J.: Princeton University Press, 1956), 468.
30 Jesse A. Tolerton to Herbert S. Hadley, November 18, 1914, Herbert S. Hadley Papers, University of Missouri, Columbia.
31 Wilson to Oscar W. Underwood, October 17, 1914, Woodrow Wilson Papers, Manuscript Division, Library of Congress.
32 Woodrow Wilson to Powell Evans, October 20, 1914, in Link, ed., *The Papers of Woodrow Wilson, Volume 31*, 187.
33 Ray Stannard Baker, *American Chronicle: The Autobiography of Ray Stannard Baker* (New York: Charles Scribner's Sons), 277.
34 *Washington Post*, November 7, 1914.
35 Tumulty to Wilson, December 4, 1914, in, Link, ed., *The Papers of Woodrow Wilson, Volume 31*, 389.
36 "An Annual Message to Congress," in Link, ed., *The Papers of Woodrow Wilson, Volume 31*, 415; "Mr. Wilson to Congress," *New York Times*, December 9, 1914.
37 Woodrow Wilson to William McAdoo, November 17, 1914, in "President Sees New America," *New York Times*, November 18, 1914.
38 Link, *The New Freedom*, 471.
39 "Show Them His Promised Boom," New York, *Sun*, December 27, 1914.
40 "Congress Must Place U.S. upon Fighting Basis," *Washington Herald*, October 16, 1914.
41 *New York Times*, October 20, 1914.
42 William C. Widenor, *Henry Cabot Lodge and the Search for an American Foreign Policy* (Berkeley: University of California Press, 1980), 200–291; Justus Doenecke, *Nothing Less Than War: A New History of America's Entry into World War I* (Lexington: University of Kentucky Press, 2011), 34–36.
43 See Wilson annual message, December 8, 1914, Link, ed., *The Papers of Woodrow Wilson, Volume 31*, 423.
44 Gardner was quoted in Pendleton, Oregon, *East Oregonian*, December 11, 1914; James T. Williams, Jr., to Theodore Roosevelt, December 15, 1914, Williams, Jr. Papers.
45 "Bitter Fight Opens on Shipping Bill," *New York Times*, January 15, 1915.
46 S. R. Honey to John St. Loe Strachey, January 9, 1915, Box 26, John St. Loe Strachey Papers, House of Lords Record Office, London.
47 "Two-Edged Inquiry Voted," *New York Times*, February 16, 1915.
48 Lodge to Roosevelt, February 11, 1915, Roosevelt Papers.

49 "President Wilson's Speech," *New York Times*, January 9, 1915.

50 "See Wilson Threat," *Washington Post*, January 10, 1915.

51 Lodge to Roosevelt, January 15, 1915, Roosevelt Papers.

52 Wilson to Nancy Saunders Toy, February 4, 1915, in Link, ed., *The Papers of Woodrow Wilson, Volume 32*, 191.

CHAPTER THREE. THE REPUBLICAN FIELD

1 Henry L. Stoddard to Francis B. Loomis, April 20, 1915, Francis B. Loomis Papers, Stanford University Library. George Harvey, "the Bases of Republican Confidence," *The North American Review* 201 (February 1915): 711–725, considered the electoral prospects of both parties after the 1914 elections. William H. Osborn Diary, December 27, 1914, Joyner Library, East Carolina University, Greenville, North Carolina.

2 "Why Not the Republican Candidate?," *Independent* 84 (November 29, 1915): 331–332.

3 William Howard Taft to Myron Herrick, December 14, 1914, Taft to Mrs. Buckner Wallingford, May 25, 1915, William Howard Taft Papers, Manuscript Division, Library of Congress.

4 Theodore Roosevelt to Hiram Johnson, November 6, 1914, Roosevelt to William Allen White, November 7, 1914, Roosevelt to Susan Dexter Dalton Cooley, December 2, 1914, Theodore Roosevelt Papers, Manuscript Division, Library of Congress.

5 Historians for years dismissed the charges as Allied propaganda, but modern scholars find them valid. See John Horne and Alan Kramer, *German Atrocities, 1914: A History of Denial* (New Haven, Conn.: Yale University Press, 2001).

6 "Roosevelt for War," *Washington Post*, August 22, 1915.

7 *The Letters of Theodore Roosevelt*, Elting E. Morison et al., eds., 8 vols. (Cambridge, Mass.: Harvard University Press, 1951–1954), 8: 922, note 1. Roosevelt's statement is given in the editorial note.

8 Philip C. Jessup, *Elihu Root*, 2 vols. (New York: Dodd Mead, 1938), 2: 309–323, is good on Root and World War I.

9 William Howard Taft to Gus Karger, June 17, 1915, Taft Papers.

10 Myron T. Herrick to William McKinley, February 24, 1898, William McKinley Papers, Manuscript Division, Library of Congress, and George B. Cortelyou Diary, May 22, 1898, Box 52, George B. Cortelyou Papers, Manuscript Division, Library of Congress, are illuminating on Herrick's closeness to President McKinley.

11 Marcus A. Hanna to Theodore Roosevelt, December 23, 1903, Roosevelt Papers. Elihu Root to Myron Herrick, August 24, 1912, Elihu Root Papers, Manuscript Division, Library of Congress.

12 "New Envoy Sails on August 8," *New York Times*, July 31, 1914.

13 "Urge That Herrick Stay," *New York Times*, November 11, 1914.

14 T. Bentley Mott, *Myron Herrick, Friend of France* (Garden City, N.Y.: Doubleday, Doran, 1929), 243.

15 "Persons in the Foreground: Mr. Herrick and His Disinherited Presidential Boom," *Current Opinion* (January 1915): 3.

16 The best source on Weeks is Benjamin Arthur Spence, "The National Career of John Wingate Weeks (1904–1925)" (PhD diss.: The University of Wisconsin, 1971). See also Charles G. Washburn, *The Life of John W. Weeks* (Boston: Houghton Mifflin, 1928).

17 John Wingate Weeks to Henry L. Higginson, April 29, 1910, Henry L. Higginson Papers, Baker Library, Harvard University.

18 Week to Higginson, February 17, 1911, Higginson Papers.

19 Theodore Roosevelt to Charles G. Washburn, June 23, 1915, Roosevelt Papers.

20 "New Commission Has Great Power," Ogden City, Utah, *Ogden Standard*, March 11, 1915; "Writes Doom of Democracy," *Los Angeles Times*, April 7, 1915; "Weeks Sees Burton, Root and Himself as Possible Candidates," *Washington Post*, May 6, 1915.

21 Ashmun Brown to Erastus Brainerd, February 3, 1916, Erastus Brainerd Papers, University of Washington Library, Seattle.

22 James T. Williams, Jr., to Frank H. Hitchcock, May 16, 1916, James T. Williams, Jr. Papers, Duke University Library, Durham, North Carolina.

23 William R. Knight, "Senator Cummins of Iowa," *Los Angeles Times*, May 9, 1915.

24 Nancy C. Unger, *Fighting Bob La Follette: The Righteous Reformer* (Chapel Hill: University of North Carolina Press, 2000), 235.

25 Edward Brundage to Lawrence Yates Sherman, January 8, 1916, Box 37, Lawrence Yates Sherman Papers, Abraham Lincoln Presidential Library, Springfield, Illinois.

26 Joseph B. Kealing to Charles W. Fairbanks, April 12, 1916, Charles W. Fairbanks Papers, Lilly Library, Indiana University, Bloomington, Indiana, discusses the chances of Fairbanks at the impending national convention.

27 Hughes told his own story in a series of biographical notes that were well edited by David J. Danelski and Joseph S. Tulchin, *The Autobiographical Notes of Charles Evans Hughes* (Cambridge, Mass.: Harvard University Press, 1973). The only full biography is Merlo Pusey, *Charles Evans Hughes*, 2 vols. (New York: Macmillan, 1951). James F. Simon, *FDR and Chief Justice Hughes: The President, the Supreme Court and the Epic Battle over the New Deal* (New York: Simon & Schuster, 2012), is an interesting comparative study with useful background information on Hughes. Robert F. Wesser, *Charles Evans Hughes: Politics and Reform in New York State, 1905–1910* (Ithaca, N.Y.: Cornell University Press, 1967), is the reliable account of Hughes as governor of New York. A new biography of Hughes would be a useful contribution.

28 Danelski and Tulchin, *Autobiographical Notes*, 44.

29 Gherardi Davis to Theodore Roosevelt, July 29, 1906, Gherardi Davis Papers, New York Public Library, Astor, Lenox and Tilden Foundations.

30 Richard L. McCormick, *From Realignment to Reform: Political Change in New York State, 1893–1910* (Ithaca, N.Y.: Cornell University Press, 1981), 221.

31 Eugene G. Hay to Louis T. Michener, October 22, 1906, Eugene G. Hay Papers, Manuscript Division, Library of Congress.

32 Elihu Root to John Coit Spooner, October 30, 1906, John Coit Spooner Papers, Manuscript Division, Library of Congress.

33 Jessup, *Elihu Root*, 2: 120.

34 Nicholas Murray Butler to Root, November 7, 1906, Nicholas Murray Butler Papers, Columbia University Library, New York.

35 Robert H. Fuller to Henry L. Higginson, April 10, 1908, Higginson Papers.

36 William A. Barnes to Elihu Root, January 27, 1909, Root Papers.

37 The reporters asked "Is the President Hostile to the Hughes Boom?" *Literary Digest* 35 (November 30, 1907): 814–816.

38 Roosevelt to Kermit Roosevelt, January 27, 1908, Roosevelt Papers.

39 Mark Sullivan, *Our Times: 1900–1925. Volume 4: The War Begins, 1909–1914* (New York: Scribner, 1936), 304. For other reaction to Hughes and his principles, see George von Lengerke Meyer Diary, February 1, 1908, Manuscript Division, Library of Congress.

40 Elbert F. Baldwin to Theodore Roosevelt, June 19, 1908, Roosevelt Papers, conveying the refusal of Hughes to take the second spot. Pusey, *Hughes*, 1: 239, has the text of Baldwin's telegram to Hughes.

41 Meyer Diary, August 20, 1908.

42 "Gov. Hughes Speaks for Taft in Ohio," *New-York Tribune*, September 6, 1908.

43 *Hughes' Reply to Bryan: Governor of New York Demolishes Democratic Candidate's arguments in Speech at Youngstown, O. Sep., 5, 1908* (Chicago: Allied Printing, 1908), 7, pamphlet in author's collection.

44 Ibid., 11–12.

45 Ibid., 22.

46 Ibid., 26.

47 *New-York Tribune*, September 7, 1908.

48 Republican National Committee, *Republican Campaign Text-Book, 1916* (Washington, D.C.: Republican National Committee, 1916), 43.

49 "The Intellectual Quality of Hughes," New York, *Sun*, September 6, 1908.

50 Louis T. Michener to Chester I. Long, September 5, 1908, Chester I. Long Papers, Kansas State Historical Society, Topeka.

51 "Chanler Now Puts Questions to Hughes," *New York Times*, October 20, 1908.

52 "Mack Assails Hughes," *Washington Post*, June 12, 1916.

53 See, for example, Frederick C. Stevens to William Howard Taft, June 16, 1912, Charles D. Hilles Papers, Sterling Memorial Library, Yale University, New Haven, Connecticut.

54 Lewis L. Gould, "Almost Lawyer Presidents," in Norman Gross, ed., *America's Lawyer Presidents: Updated Edition* (Evanston, IL: Northwestern University Press, 2009), 318, quotes Hughes.

55 See "Why Not the Republican Candidate?" *Independent*, 84 (November 29,

1915): 331–333, setting forth why Hughes would make a good Republican nominee.

56 "Hughes Talk," Denison, Iowa, *Denison Review*, March 24, 1915.

CHAPTER FOUR. THE STATE OF THE DEMOCRATS

1 "A Republican View," *North American Review* 201 (April 1915): 713, expressed the Republican position.

2 Franklin K. Lane to John Crawford Burns, March 3, 1915, in Anne Wintermute Lane and Louis Herrick Wall, eds., *The Letters of Franklin K. Lane* (Boston and New York: Houghton Mifflin, 1922), 167.

3 Albert S. Burleson to William V. Judson, March 30, 1915, Albert S. Burleson Papers, Manuscript Division, Library of Congress.

4 Thomas J. Pence to Fred B. Lynch, December 7, 1914, Josiah Bailey Papers, Duke University Library; Pence to Claude Kitchin, January 6, 1916, Claude Kitchin Papers, Southern Historical Collection, University of North Carolina Library.

5 "Wilson to Give Cue," *Washington Post*, October 31, 1915. For a restatement of the Republican position, see "The Discredited Democratic Party," *Washington Post*, March 24, 1915, and for a contrasting view, "Business Trenches 'Retaken,'" *Literary Digest* 50 (April 17, 1915): 859–860.

6 William Howard Taft to Charles P. Taft, June 12, 1915, William Howard Taft Papers, Manuscript Division, Library of Congress.

7 "Party Leaders Have No Fear of a Split," *Washington Post*, June 10, 1915.

8 Kristie Miller, *Ellen and Edith: Woodrow Wilson's First Ladies* (Lawrence: University Press of Kansas, 2010), 108–132, is excellent on Wilson's courtship of Edith Galt.

9 "Wilson's Hat in Ring, Washington Thinks," *New York Times*, January 10, 1915.

10 "Wilson Seems Choice," *Washington Post*, May 28, 1915.

11 "Wilson Looks to 1916," *Washington Post*, August 11, 1915.

12 "Wilson to Give Clue," *Washington Post*, October 31, 1915.

13 Cecil Spring Rice to Edward Grey, December 9, 1915, FO371/2501/195872, British National Archives, Kew.

14 "G.O.P. Year, Says Taft," *Washington Post*, November 21, 1915; "Democrats See Bull Moose Drift," *New York Times*, November 4, 1915.

15 Wilson to Charles A. Culberson, May 5, 1916, *New York Times*, May 5, 1916. Melvin I. Urofsky, *Louis D. Brandeis; A Life* (New York: Pantheon, 2009), 433–459, is an informed view of the battle over the Brandeis nomination.

16 F. E. Scobey to Warren G. Harding, February 19, 1916, Warren G. Harding Papers, Ohio Historical Society, Columbus. For a full discussion of the tariff commission issue, see Karen Schnietz, "Democrats 1916 Tariff Commission: Responding to Dumping Fears and Illustrating the Consumer Costs of Protectionism," *Business History Review* 72 (Spring, 1998): 1–45.

17 Franklin K. Lane to Wilson, June 8, 1916, The Papers of Woodrow Wilson, Manuscript Division, Library of Congress.

18 *New Republic* 1 (January 16, 1915): 3–4.

19 Herbert Croly, "Unregenerate Democracy," *New Republic* 6 (February 5, 1916): 19.

20 Theodore Roosevelt to Arthur Lee, January 27, 1916, Lee Papers, Courtauld Institute, London.

21 William Jennings Bryan to Josephus Daniels, February 4, 1916, in Paolo Coletta, vol. 3 of *William Jennings Bryan* (Lincoln, Neb.: University of Nebraska Press, 1964–1969), 17.

22 "Nation Blindly Stumbling toward War, Says Root," *New-York Tribune*, February 16, 1916.

23 Eric Drummond to Edward Grey, February 18, 1916, FO800/105, Edward Grey Papers, British National Archives, Kew.

24 Joseph Tumulty to Woodrow Wilson, February 18, 1916, Woodrow Wilson Papers, Manuscript Division, Library of Congress.

25 "Ex-Governor Glynn's Speech; Dissects Root's Address Here and Replies to His Attacks," *New York Times*, March 2, 1916. For background on Glynn, see Dominick C. Lizzi, *Forgotten Hero: Governor Martin H. Glynn* (Valatie, N.Y.: Valatie Press, 2007).

26 "Ex-Governor Glynn's Speech."

27 Ibid.

28 Ibid.

29 F. Dixon to Locock, February 15, 1916, Papers of Lord Cecil of Charnwood, BL51092, British Library, London.

30 For speech preparations, see Martin Glynn to Joseph Tumulty, May 6, 1916, Series 4, Case File 3233, Wilson Papers.

31 Edward M. House to E. S. Martin, August 30, 1911, Edward M. House Papers, Sterling Memorial Library, Yale University. Charles E. Neu, *Colonel House: A Biography of Woodrow Wilson's Silent Partner* (New York: Oxford University Press, 2015), is the biography that House has long needed and is essential for understanding his friendship with the president.

32 House to Sidney Mezes, November 25, 1911, House Papers.

33 For information on McCormick, see Bellefonte, Pennsylvania, *Democratic Watchman*, June 23, 1916, and "McCormick Chosen Wilson's Manager," *Washington Times*, June 15, 1916. Information on McCormick is available online at the McCormick Family Papers website through Pennsylvania Culture Studies.

34 For a modern analysis that somewhat overstates Woolley's influence, see Dan Balz and John Maxwell Hamilton, "In 2016, We're Going to Campaign Like It's 1916," *Washington Post*, January 2, 2015, www.washingtonpost.com/opinions/in-2016-were going to campaign-like-its-1916. Mark Hanna in 1896 and 1900 and George B. Cortelyou in 1904 would have been surprised to learn that they were not engaged attracting specific ethnic and religious groups within the electorate in their campaigns.

35 Edward House to Woodrow Wilson, July 25, 1916, Wilson Papers.

36 Thomas J. Walsh to Vance McCormick, August 10, 1916, Box 172, Thomas J. Walsh Papers, Library of Congress.

37 William J. Stone to Joseph Tumulty, November 11, 1915, Series 4, Case File 2621, Wilson Papers.

38 George B. Lockwood to Charles W. Fairbanks, May 23, 1916, Charles W. Fairbanks Papers, Lilly Library, Indiana University, Bloomington, Indiana.

39 "Democratic Party Platform of 1916," www.presidency.ucsb.edu/ws/?pid=2591.

40 Ibid.

41 "Democracy in Dreamland," *The Outlook* (June 28, 1916): 453.

42 Martin Green, "Glynn's Eulogy of Wilson and Peace Stirs Whirlwind in Convention," New York, *World*, June 14, 1916.

43 Gus J. Karger to William Howard Taft, June 29, 1916, Taft Papers.

44 "Democracy in Dreamland," 453.

45 George Harvey, "The National Conventions," *North American Review* 204 (July 1916): 738. The classic account of the Democratic convention is in Arthur S. Link, *Wilson: Campaigns for Progressivism and Peace, 1916–1917* (Princeton, N.J: Princeton University Press, 1965), 38–48.

46 "Which?" New York, *World*, June 19, 1916.

CHAPTER FIVE. THE SELECTION OF HUGHES AND THE LAUNCHING OF THE REPUBLICAN CAMPAIGN

1 Henry L. Stimson Diary, May 19, 1916, Henry L. Stimson Papers, Sterling Memorial Library, Yale University, New Haven.

2 Lewis L. Gould, *The Republicans: A History of the Grand Old Party* (New York: Oxford University Press, 2014), considers the underlying assumptions about Republican legitimacy.

3 James T. Williams, Jr., to Frank Hitchcock, March 7, 1916, Williams to C. F. Ellefson, April 6, 1915, James T. Williams, Jr. Papers, Duke University Library, discuss the problems with Roosevelt as a presidential candidate.

4 Gus Karger to William Howard Taft, June 2, 1916, William Howard Taft Papers, Manuscript Division, Library of Congress.

5 Roosevelt's statement appears in Elting E. Morison et al., eds., *The Letters of Theodore Roosevelt*, 8 vols. (Cambridge, Mass.: Harvard University Press, 1951–1954), 8: 1024–1026.

6 "Roosevelt's Defence Plea Rouses West," *New-York Tribune*, May 31, 1916. The text of Roosevelt's remarks appeared on page 4.

7 "Hughes Strongest, Old Guard Admits," *New York Times*, June 7, 1916.

8 These arrangements are discussed in John A. Garraty, *Right-Hand Man; The Life of George W. Perkins* (New York: Harper & Bros., 1957, 1960), 332–351. The best discussion of Roosevelt in 1916 occurs in John Allen Gable, *The Bull Moose Years: Theodore Roosevelt and the Progressive Party* (Port Washington, N.Y.: Kennikat Press, 1978).

9 Theodore Roosevelt to Arthur Lee, June 7, 1916, Papers of Lord Lee of Fareham, Courtauld Institute, London.

10 William Allen White, *The Autobiography of William Allen White* (New York: Macmillan, 1946), 527.

11 "Put Hughes Boom in Concrete Form," *New York Times,* June 6, 1916.

12 "Two Lead with G.O. P.," *Washington Post,* April 3, 1916, quoting the New York *Herald.*

13 "Hitchcock Explains Activity for Hughes," *New York Times,* June 5, 1916; James T. Williams, Jr. to Frank Hitchcock, May 16, 1916, Williams, Jr. Papers.

14 William Howard Taft to Charles Evans Hughes, April 11, 1916, in Merlo Pusey, *Charles Evans Hughes,* 2 vols. (New York: Macmillan, 1951), 1: 318–319.

15 Republican National Committee, *Republican Campaign Text-Book 1916* (Washington, D.C.: Republican National Committee, 1916), 20, 27; Dudley Field Malone to Woodrow Wilson, June 7, 1916, Edward M. House to Wilson, June 7, 1916, in Arthur S. Link et al., eds., *The Papers of Woodrow Wilson, Volume 37: May 9–August 7, 1916* (Princeton, N.J.: Princeton University Press, 1981), 167–168.

16 "Whitman Puts Hughes' Name in Nomination," *Washington Times,* June 9, 1916.

17 Charles Fairbanks to Victor Rosewater, June 26, 1916, Victor Rosewater Papers, American Jewish Historical Society, Cincinnati.

18 Warren G. Harding to Charles Evans Hughes, June 10, 1916, wired the Justice official word of his selection, Charles Evans Hughes Papers, Manuscript Division, Library of Congress. An interesting contemporary assessment of Hughes and his attitude toward the potential Republican nomination is T. G. Joslin to James T. Williams, Jr., July 1916, Williams, Jr. Papers; it broadly tracks the conclusions of Pusey, *Hughes,* 1: 326–328.

19 Charles Evans Hughes to Warren G. Harding, June 10, 1916, *Republican Campaign Text-Book,* 30–31. Henry Cabot Lodge to Hughes, June 11, 1916, and James E. Watson to Hughes, June 13, 1916, Hughes Papers, were among the congratulatory messages the nominee received.

20 *New-York Tribune,* June 11, 1916.

21 George Wickersham to William Howard Taft, June 14, 1916, Taft Papers.

22 Nicholas Murray Butler to James Bryce, June 16, 1916, James Bryce American Correspondence, Bodleian Library, Oxford, England.

23 "'They're Off!' At the Hughes Headquarters," *New York Times,* June 18, 1916.

24 Ibid.

25 For anti-Hitchcock letters, see Walter S. Dickey to Charles Evans Hughes, June 13, 1916, R. W. Austin to William M. Calder, June 14, 1916, and William Howard Taft to Hughes, June 13, 1916, all in Hughes Papers.

26 "Willcox Suggested as Hughes Manager," *New York Times,* June 19, 1916 (quotation); "Whitman Sees Hughes in Behalf of Willcox," New York, *World,* June 24, 1916. Nicholas Murray Butler to Charles Evans Hughes, June 27, 1916, touted Willcox, Hughes Papers. Also see "Hughes Pilot Chosen," *Washington Post,* June 28, 1916.

27 M'Liss, "Spry Mrs. Hughes Comes Up Smiling on Political Ordeal," Philadelphia *Evening Ledger,* October 10, 1916.

28 "Quaint Old Portraits in the Hughes Family Album," Washington, *Sunday Star,* July 2, 1916.

29 "Glimpse of Next First Lady of the Land," Washington, *Evening Star*, November 7, 1916.

30 David J. Daneski and Joseph S. Tulchin, eds., *The Autobiographical Notes of Charles Evans Hughes* (Cambridge, Mass.: Harvard University Press, 1973), 200; for more information on Willcox, see "Persons in the Foreground: The Ph.B And The L.L.D. Who Are to Run the Presidential Campaign," *Current Opinion* 61 (August 1916): 91, 92.

31 Edward M. House to Woodrow Wilson, June 28, 1916, in Link et al., eds., *The Papers of Woodrow Wilson, Volume 37*, 320.

32 Woodrow Wilson to Edward House, July 2, 1916, in Link et al., eds., *The Papers of Woodrow Wilson, Volume 37*, 346.

33 "Campaign's First Figures Give Wilson 16 Majority in the Electoral College," New York, *World*, August 8, 1916. The *World*, as the leading Democratic newspaper in the country, is a good indicator of the basic strength of the Hughes campaign as the canvass began.

34 "Women Win Hughes to Amendment," *New York Times*, August 2, 1916. His public declaration occurred in a telegram to Senator George Sutherland, August 1, 1916, Hughes Papers.

35 Gus Karger to William Howard Taft, July 19, 1916, Taft Papers.

36 Gus Karger to William Howard Taft, June 29, 1916, Taft Papers.

37 Gus Karger to William Howard Taft, July 19, 1916, Taft Papers.

38 "Great Throng Cheers Hughes as He Accepts," *New-York Tribune*, August 1, 1916.

39 "Charles E. Hughes Speech of Acceptance at Carnegie Hall, New York," July 31, 1916," *Republican Campaign Text-Book*, 4.

40 Ibid.

41 Myron T. Herrick to Charles Evans Hughes, August 1, 1916, Alexander P. Moore to Hughes, August 1, 1916, John Hays Hammond to Hughes, August 1, 1916, Charles W. Fairbanks to Hughes, August 2, 1916, Hughes Papers, provide initial Republican reactions to the acceptance speech.

42 "Cabinet Derides Hughes Speech; Keynote Welcomed by Republicans," *Washington Times*, August 1, 1916.

43 Norman Hapgood, "Is Hughes Going Down Hill," *Independent* 87 (August 21, 1915), 272.

44 Walter Lippmann to Newton Baker, August 2, 1916, in Link et al., eds., *The Papers of Woodrow Wilson, Volume 37*, 525.

45 T. G. Joslin to James T. Williams, Jr., July 10, 1916, Williams, Jr. Papers.

46 "Hughes Will Pose for Movie Camera," *Washington Times*, July 2, 1916.

47 "I'm Perfectly Human, Says Hughes, Nettled," *Washington Herald*, August 2, 1916. An early example of the effort to humanize Hughes was John Palmer Gavit, "Charles Evans Hughes, the Man; Sidelights on the Personality of the Former Governor of New York," *New York Evening Post*, June 10, 1916, republished as a pamphlet (New York: The Nation Press, 1916).

48 Theodore Roosevelt to Charles Evans Hughes, August 11, 1916, Theodore Roosevelt Papers, Manuscript Division, Library of Congress.

49 The decision to identify with regular, conservative Republicans and to stay out of factional fights would, of course, have large consequences for Hughes and what became the crucial electoral vote of California. The interaction between Hughes and Hiram Johnson has been the subject of historical scrutiny for years. The basic sources for understanding what happened include Alfred Holman, "The Case of Hiram Johnson, Guilty," *North American Review* 205 (February 1917): 186 ff.; Frederick M. Davenport, "The Case of Hiram Johnson, Not Guilty," *North American Review* 205 (February 1917): 203–220. Davenport fleshed out his earlier account in "Did Hughes Snub Johnson?—An Inside Story, How and Why Charles Evans Hughes Lost California and the Presidency in 1916," *American Political Science Review* 43 (April 1949): 321–332. The best historical account is Spencer Olin, "Hiram Johnson, the California Progressives and the Hughes Campaign of 1916," *Pacific Historical Review* 31 (November 1962): 403–412.

50 E. Dana Durand to Charles Evans Hughes, August 9, 1917 (1916), Hughes Papers.

51 "Hughes Preaches Tariff on Coast," *Washington Herald*, August 17, 1916.

52 Benjamin B. Lindsey to Theodore Roosevelt, August 30, 1916, Roosevelt Papers.

53 Davenport, "An Inside Story," 325 (emphasis in the original); "Labor Official Attacks Hughes," *Washington Herald*, August 20, 1916.

54 "Hughes Speech Angers Moose," *New-York Tribune*, August 20, 1916.

55 Meyer Lissner to Theodore Roosevelt, August 28, 1916, Roosevelt Papers.

56 "Hughes Resting High in Rockies," *Washington Herald*, August 28, 1916 (second quotation); "Hitchcock Back in Republican Campaign," *Washington Herald*, August 31, 1916.

57 H. V. Jones to Theodore Roosevelt, September 1, 1916, Roosevelt Papers.

58 "The End of a Legend," *New York Times*, August 10, 1916.

59 Herman Wise to William McAdoo, August 14, 1916, Woodrow Wilson Papers, Manuscript Division, Library of Congress.

60 Nicholas Woods to Woodrow Wilson, August 16, 1916, Wilson Papers.

61 "Say Willcox May Go," *Washington Post*, September 3, 1916.

62 "Willcox to Stay as G.O.P. Head," *Washington Herald*, September 3, 1916.

CHAPTER SIX. THE CAMPAIGN BECOMES IDEOLOGICAL

1 Ray Stannard Baker, *Woodrow Wilson: Life and Letters, Facing War, 1915–1917* (New York: Charles Scribner's Sons, 1937, 1946), 267.

2 Arthur S. Link et al., eds., *The Papers of Woodrow Wilson, Volume 37: May 9–August 7, 1916* (Princeton, N.J.: Princeton University Press, 1981), 116.

3 Richard Stockton to Joseph P. Tumulty, August 25, 1916, Series 4, Case File 3249, Woodrow Wilson Papers, Manuscript Division, Library of Congress.

4 Arthur S. Link et al., eds., *The Papers of Woodrow Wilson, Volume 38: August 7–November 19, 1916* (Princeton, N.J.: Princeton University Press, 1982), 131.

5 Ibid., 127 (second quotation), 133.

6 Ibid., 138.

7 Link et al., eds., *The Papers of Woodrow Wilson, Volume 38*, 139.

8 "The President's Defense of His Record," *Literary Digest* 53 (September 16, 1916): 654.

9 Ibid.

10 "Mr. Wilson Accepts the Nomination," *Washington Herald*, September 3, 1916; "Reckoning and Assessment," *New York Times*, September 3, 1916.

11 "Head Coach for the Democrats," *Life* 68 (July 20, 1916): 120.

12 John J. McCarron to Thomas J. Walsh, September 25, 1916, Box 172, Thomas J. Walsh Papers, Library of Congress; the pamphlet titles are listed in Arthur S. Link, *Wilson: Campaigns for Progressivism and Peace* (Princeton, N.J.: Princeton University Press, 1965), 98; Edward M. House to Woodrow Wilson, October 5, 1916, Wilson Papers.

13 Michael E. McGerr, *The Decline of Popular Politics: The American North, 1865–1928* (New York: Oxford University Press, 1986), 164–167, is good on Woolley in the campaign.

14 Arthur Willert to Geoffrey [Robinson] Dawson, October 14, 1916, Archives of *The Times*, London.

15 San Francisco *Leader*, February 26, 1916, quoted in William M. Leary, Jr., "Woodrow Wilson, Irish Americans and the Election of 1916," *Journal of American History* 54 (June 1967): 60.

16 Link et al., eds., *The Papers of Woodrow Wilson, Volume 38*, 97.

17 "Hughes in New England Assails 8-Hour Act," Washington, *Evening Star*, September 7, 1916.

18 Charles Evans Hughes to William Howard Taft, September 16, 1916, Taft Papers.

19 "Political Effects of the Labor Victory," *Literary Digest* 53 (September 16, 1915): 652 (both quotations).

20 Charles D. Hilles to William Howard Taft, September 26, 1916, Taft Papers.

21 Charles Sumner Bird to Charles Evans Hughes, September 12, 1916, Robert R. McCormick to Hughes, October 2, 1916, Charles Evans Hughes Papers, Manuscript Division, Library of Congress.

22 Joseph Hodges Choate, "Hot Shot Poured into Wilson Administration" (New York: Freytag Press, 1916), pamphlet in author's collection. Choate was one of the few Republicans who expected Wilson to be reelected. See Choate to Lord Grey, June 26, 1916, Papers of the 4th Earl Grey, Department of Paleographic and Diplomatic, University of Durham, England.

23 Clarence Wood, "Fears for Democracy," *New-York Tribune*, September 4, 1916.

24 "Eight-Hour Law Campaign Issue," Washington, *Evening Star*, September 5, 1916; "Wilsonism and Its Appeal," *New-York Tribune*, October 16, 1916.

25 Lawrence Y. Sherman to Charles G. Dawes, September 10, 1916, Henry M. Dawes to Sherman, September 7, 1916, Box 38, Correspondence August–December 1916, Lawrence Y. Sherman Papers, Abraham Lincoln Presidential Library, Springfield, Illinois. I am indebted to Tim Mottaz for locating these references for me.

26 James T. Willams, Jr., to "Mr. Ford," September 14, 1916, James T. Williams, Jr. Papers, Duke University Library; "The President's Defense of His Record," *Literary Digest* 53 (September 16, 1916): 655.

27 Lemuel R. Quigg to Theodore Roosevelt, September 13, 1916, Theodore Roosevelt Papers, Manuscript Division, Library of Congress.

28 Benjamin Richmond to William Willcox, September 13, 1916, Hughes Papers.

29 "What He Stands For," New York, *Sun*, November 2, 1916.

30 "Wilson a Failure, Says Root," *New York Times*, October 6, 1916.

31 Gus Karger to William Howard Taft, September 4, 1916, Taft Papers.

32 T. G. Joslin to James T. Williams, Jr., September 3, 1916, Williams, Jr. Papers.

33 Charles Evans Hughes to Theodore Roosevelt, September 15, 1916, Hughes Papers; see for similar sentiments, Hughes to William Howard Taft, September 16, 1916, Taft Papers.

34 T. G. Joslin to James T. Williams, Jr., September 1, 1916, Williams Papers.

35 "Wilson Worse Than Pontius Pilate—TR," *Washington Herald*, September 1, 1916.

36 Taft Likens 1916 to 1896," *New York Times*, October 4, 1916.

37 "Hughes Repeats Attacks," *New York Times*, October 4, 1916.

38 "'Theodore' Grasps the Hand of 'Will,'" *New York Times*, October 4, 1916. That was not the first time that Roosevelt used that specific language. In his discussion of boxing as a sport in his autobiography, Roosevelt had written: "I do not like to see young Christians with shoulders that slope like a champagne bottle." Theodor Roosevelt, *Autobiography: The Works of Theodore Roosevelt*, 20 vols. (New York: Charles Scribner's Sons, 1926), 20: 45.

39 Theodore Roosevelt to William Willcox, September 13, 1916, Roosevelt Papers.

40 "T. R. Crushes Triple Photo," *New-York Tribune*, September 30, 1916.

41 *New-York Tribune*, September 5, 1916.

42 "Roosevelt Hits Eight-Hour Law," *New York Times*, October 1, 1916.

43 "Seven Roosevelt Speeches Pledged," *New York Times*, October 10, 1916.

44 "Roosevelt Draws Kentucky Crowd," *New York Times*, October 19, 1916.

45 Gus Karger to William Howard Taft, October 16, 1916, Taft Papers.

46 Robert R. McCormick to Charles Evans Hughes, October 2, 1916, Hughes Papers.

47 Frank Vanderlip, Henry Stimson et al., to Charles Evans Hughes, October 18, 1916, Hughes Papers.

48 David Sarasohn, *The Party of Reform: Democrats in the Progressive Era* (Jackson: University Press of Mississippi, 1989), 201, 202.

49 "Hughes Aspires to Lead Patriots," *New York Times*, October 29, 1916.

50 Ibid.

51 Woodrow Wilson to Mary Allen Hulbert, September 29, 1912, in Arthur S. Link et al., eds., *The Papers of Woodrow Wilson, Volume 25, 1912* (Princeton, N.J.: Princeton University Press, 1978), 285, shows Wilson's awareness of rumors in that year. William Allen White, *The Autobiography of William Allen*

White (New York: Macmillan, 1946), 493; Roosevelt's remark in 1916 is in John A. Garraty, *Right-hand Man: The Life of George W. Perkins* (New York: Harper & Bros., 1957, 1960), 347.

52 Woodrow Wilson to Joseph Tumulty, October 1916, Wilson Papers. See also W.W. Morris, October 21, 1916, Wilson Papers.

53 Stockton Axson, "Mr. Wilson as Seen by One of His Family Circle," *New York Times*, October 8, 1916. For the arrangement of the Ida Tarbell interview, see Woodrow Wilson to Ida Tarbell, October 3, 1916, Ida Tarbell Papers, Allegheny College.

54 Woodrow Wilson to Garrett Droppers, December 12, 1916, in Link et al., eds., *The Papers of Woodrow Wilson, Volume 40, 1916–1917* (Princeton, N.J., Princeton University Press, 1982), 219.

CHAPTER SEVEN. THE FINAL MONTH

1 Theodore H. Price and Richard Spillane, "Stalking for Nine Million Votes," *World's Work* 32 (October 1916): 663–677. The authors reported that the Democrats had ordered 450,000 Wilson buttons. The best scholarly treatment of campaign methods in 1916 is Michael E. McGerr, *The Decline of Popular Politics: The American North, 1865–1928* (New York: Oxford University Press, 1986), 162–168.

2 Daniel C. Roper to Edward M. House, October 9, 1916, Papers of Edward M. House, Sterling Memorial Library, Yale University, New Haven.

3 "An Address in Atlantic City to the National American Woman Suffrage Association," September 8, 1916, in Arthur S. Link et al., eds., *The Papers of Woodrow Wilson, Volume 38 , August 7, 1916–November 19, 1916* (Princeton, N.J.: Princeton University Press, 1982), 163. See also Alice Chipman Dewey to Norman Hapgood, September 14, 1916, in *The Papers of Woodrow Wilson, Volume 38*, 175–176.

4 " A Campaign Speech at Shadow Lawn," September 23, 1916, in Link, et al., eds., *The Papers of Woodrow Wilson, Volume 38*, 212–219.

5 "A Campaign Speech to Young Democrats at Shadow Lawn," in Link et al., eds., *The Papers of Woodrow Wilson, Volume 38*, 306.

6 "Wilson and Peace or Hughes and War Campaign Slogan," New York, *World*, October 2, 1916.

7 "'Man of Peace' Shouts Hughes," *Washington Herald*, October 15, 1916.

8 Arthur S. Link, *Wilson: Campaigns for Progressivism and Peace* (Princeton, N.J.: Princeton University Press, 1965), 114.

9 O'Leary presented his version of the telegraphic interchange in Jeremiah O'Leary and Michael Kelly, *My Political Trial and Experiences* (New York: Jefferson Publishing, 1919), 45–50. Woodrow Wilson to Jeremiah O'Leary, September 29, 1916, in Link et al., eds., *The Papers of Woodrow Wilson, Volume 38*, 286.

10 Edward M. House to Woodrow Wilson, September 30, 1916, in Link et al., eds., *The Papers of Woodrow Wilson, Volume 38*, 317.

11 Gus Karger to William Howard Taft, October 1, 1916, William Howard Taft Papers, Manuscript Division, Library of Congress.

12 G. R. Brainard to Theodore Roosevelt, October 8, 1916, Lucius B. Swift to Roosevelt, October 23, 1916, Theodore Roosevelt Papers, Library of Congress.

13 Frances A. Kellor, *Women in the Campaign* (New York: McConnell Press, 1917), a reprint of an article that originally appeared in the *Yale Review* in January 1917. See also Frances Kellor to Elizabeth Freeman, August 17, 1916, August 31, 1916, in "An Interactive Scrapbook of Elizabeth Freeman: Suffragette, Civil Rights Worker and Militant Pacifist," www.elizabethfreeman.org. This online archive has valuable documents about the Hughes campaign train and its female riders.

14 Albert J. Beveridge to Mrs. Beveridge, October 8, 1916, in Claude G. Bowers, *Beveridge and the Progressive Era* (Boston: Houghton Mifflin, 1932), 493. J. Leonard Bates and Vanette M. Schwartz, "Golden Special Campaign Train: Republican Women Campaign for Charles Evans Hughes for President in 1916," *Montana: The Magazine of Western History* 37 Summer 1987): 26–35, is a good account of the train.

15 "Hughesettes 'Egged' by Crowd in Chicago," *The Washington Herald*, November 2, 1916; "Tired Hughesettes Getting Neat Home," New York, *World*, November 3, 1916.

16 "Likens Mexicans to Boys of '76," *New-York Tribune*, October 17, 1916.

17 "Baker's Slur on '76 Heroes Is Condemned," *New-York Tribune*, October 18, 1916.

18 O. D. Knabenshue to Newton D. Baker, October 26, 1916, Box 222, Newton D. Baker Papers, Manuscript Division, Library of Congress. See also Frank J. Stupp et al., to Baker, October 1916, Ernest Fudge to Baker, October 20, 1916, Baker Papers. Fudge indicated that the stenographer at the speech failed to take down accurately what Baker said. I am indebted to Dr. Richard T. McCulley of Washington, D.C., for furnishing me with copies of these documents.

19 "Hughes Calls Baker's Slur Disgraceful," *New-York Tribune*, October 20, 1916.

20 "Demand Baker Resign Post for '76 Slurs," *New-York Tribune*, October 23, 1916.

21 "Washington's Soldiers Just as Bad Character as Mexicans," *Bismarck Daily Tribune*, October 23, 1916.

22 "Mr. Baker Denies That Villa Speech," *New York Times*, October 27, 1916. Oddly, Baker's most recent biographer has little to say about the episode in its political context, but then he ignores the election of 1916 as it applied to his subjects. Douglas B. Craig, *Progressives at War—William G. McAdoo and Newton Baker, 1863–1941* (Baltimore, Md.: Johns Hopkins University Press, 2013), 144, 147. For McAdoo's involvement in the Hughes-Wilson contest, Vance McCormick to William MacAdoo, October 23, 1916. William G. McAdoo Papers, Manuscript Division, Library of Congress. The *Tribune* editors

maintained that their reporter had quoted Baker's remarks accurately. Edwin N. Lewis to Theodore Roosevelt, October 30, 1916, Roosevelt Papers.

23 Link, *Wilson: Campaigns for Progressivism and Peace,* discusses the episode in a balanced way. William C. Widenor, *Henry Cabot Lodge and the Search for an American Foreign Policy* (Berkeley, Calif.: University of California Press, 1980), 247–248, gives Lodge's perspective. See also Henry Cabot Lodge to Theodore Roosevelt, October 30, 1916, Roosevelt Papers.

24 Link, *Wilson: Campaigns for Progressivism and Peace,* 146.

25 "Blocking Voter Fraud," *Washington Post,* October 28, 1916.

26 See Henry Lincoln Johnson, "The Negro under Wilson," in Republican National Committee, *Republican Campaign Text-Book, 1916* (Washington, D.C.: Allied Printing, 1916), 376–382.

27 Ralph Tyler to George Myers, June 16, 1916, George Myers Papers, Ohio Historical Society, Columbus.

28 John R. Lynch to George Myers, July 4, 1916, Myers Papers.

29 R. S. Hudspeth to Thomas J. Walsh, August 14, 1916, Box 172, Thomas J. Walsh Papers, Library of Congress.

30 J. M. Nimhauser to Joseph P. Tumulty, November 5, 1916, Series 4, Case File 152, Woodrow Wilson Papers, Manuscript Division, Library of Congress.

31 George E. Haynes, "Negroes Deserting South for North," *New York Times,* November 12, 1916, and "Tracing Race Exodus," *Washington Post,* October 29, 1916, were typical stories of that time.

32 "An Alarming Migration of Negro Labor," *New-York Tribune,* October 22, 1916; "Tracing Race Exodus," *Washington Post,* October 29, 1916.

33 Thomas Watt Gregory to William G. McAdoo, November 13, 1928, Thomas Watt Gregory Papers, Library of Congress, quoted in Evan Anders, "Thomas Watt Gregory and the Survival of His Progressive Faith," *Southwestern Historical Quarterly* 93 (July 1989): 12.

34 Samuel J. Graham to Woodrow Wilson, October 20, 1916, Series 4, Case File 20, Wilson Papers.

35 "Blocking Fraud Vote," *Washington Post,* October 28, 1916.

36 "Warns against Fraud," *New York Times,* November 4, 1916.

37 Elliott Rudwick, *Race Riot at East St. Louis* (Urbana: University of Illinois Press, 1964, 1982), 8–9.

38 "'Too Preposterous for Answer,' Says Miller," *Washington Herald,* October 23, 1916; "Denies Huge Vote Plot," *Washington Post,* October 23, 1916.

39 "An Address at Shadow Lawn to Wilson Volunteers," October 16, 1916, in Link et al., eds., *The Papers of Woodrow Wilson, Volume 38,* 447, 448.

40 "A Luncheon Address to Women in Cincinnati," in Link et al., eds., *The Papers of Woodrow Wilson, Volume 38,* 527.

41 "A Campaign Address to New Yorkers at Shadow Lawn," in Link et al., eds., *The Papers of Woodrow Wilson, Volume 38,* 550, 551, 555.

42 "An Interview with Henry Noble Hall," October 31, 1916, in Link et al., eds., *The Papers of Woodrow Wilson, Volume 38,* 565, 567, 570.

43 Nicholas Murray Butler to Francis B. Loomis, October, 1916, Francis B.

Loomis Papers, Stanford University; T. G. Joslin to James T. Williams, Jr., October 23, 1916, James T. Williams, Jr. Papers, Duke University.

44 Charles Evans Hughes to Charles W. Fairbanks, November 25, 1916, Charles W. Fairbanks Papers, Lilly Library, Indiana University, Bloomington.

45 "Hughes Gives His Stand, If He Is Elected," *New-York Tribune*, October 27, 1916.

46 The text of McAdoo's speech of October 18 is available in the Wilson Papers.

47 Lebbeus Wilfley to Theodore Roosevelt, October 16, 1916, Edward R. Lewis to Roosevelt, October 27, 1916, J. Cal O'Laughlin to Roosevelt, November 3, 1916, Roosevelt Papers.

48 George W. Perkins to Theodore Roosevelt, October 24, 1916, and John Sledd et al. to Roosevelt, October 24, 1916, Roosevelt Papers, for the invitation to speak at Cooper Union.

49 "T.R. Arraigns Wilson as Failure in Crisis," *New-York Tribune*, November 4, 1916.

50 "The Soul of the Nation," in *The Works of Theodore Roosevelt: Fear God and Take Your Own Part*, 20 vols. (New York: Scribner's, 1926), 18: 450, 451–452.

51 "T.R. Arraigns Wilson as Thousands Cheer"; "T.R. Riddles Wilson as Thousands Cheer, " New York, *Sun*, November 4, 1916.

52 "You Are Working;—Not Fighting! Alive and Happy—Not Cannon Fodder! Wilson and Peace with Honor or Hughes with Roosevelt and War," New York, *World*, November 4, 1916.

53 "Hughes Won't Reply," New York, *Sun*, November 6, 1916.

54 "Hughes the Favorite with Odds of 10 to 8," *Washington Herald*, November 5, 1916; Rickard is mentioned in "$50,000 Wilson Bets from West Covered," *New-York Tribune*, October 31, 1916; Paul W. Rhode and Koleman S. Stumpf, "Historical Presidential Betting Markets," *The Journal of Economic Perspectives* 18 (Spring 2004): 127–141. Rothstein of course would later be credited with fixing the 1919 World Series in the infamous "Black Sox" scandal.

55 Edward M. House Diary, November 2, 1916, Edward M. House Papers, Sterling Memorial Library, Yale University.

56 "The Broken Promise," New York, *World*, November 5, 1916; "Labor Leaders Endorse Hughes," New York, *Sun*, November 6, 1916.

57 Neil V. Salzmann, *Reform and Revolution: The Life and Times of Raymond Robins* (Kent, Ohio: Kent State University Press, 1991), 164–169.

58 Jacob Gould Schurman, "Why Progressives Want Hughes," *Independent* 88 (October 2, 1916): 14–16.

59 Walter Lippmann, "The Case for Wilson," *New Republic* 8 (October 14, 1916): 263.

60 Herbert Croly to Henry L. Stimson, October 5, 1916, Henry L. Stimson Papers, Sterling Memorial Library, Yale University, New Haven.

61 "Olney Indorses Wilson's Work; Assails Hughes," New York, *World*, September 27, 1916.

62 Woodrow Wilson to Robert Lansing, November 5, 1916, in Link et al., eds., *The Papers of Woodrow Wilson, Volume 38*, 617–618.

63 "Stevenson B. Evans, "Hughes Victory Appears Certain in Close Race," *New-York Tribune,* November 5, 1916.

64 "Hughes Forecasts His Own Election," *New-York Tribune,* November 5, 1916.

CHAPTER EIGHT. THE ELECTION AND ITS MEANING

1 Nicholas Murray Butler to Francis B. Loomis, October 23, 1916, Francis B. Loomis Papers, Stanford University.

2 William Nelson Cromwell to Charles Evans Hughes, November 8, 1916, Charles Evans Hughes Papers, Manuscript Division, Library of Congress. Robert B. Peattie, "Success Marks Hughes' Career in All Efforts," *Chicago Tribune,* November 8, 1916.

3 "'Steal Presidency at Your Peril, Warns Willcox; Only Contemptible Scoundrel Would Accuse Hughes,'" *Washington Post,* November 9, 1916.

4 Woodrow Wilson to Joseph Ruggles Wilson, November 27, 1916, Woodrow Wilson Papers, Manuscript Division, Library of Congress.

5 "The Real Answer," *New-York Tribune,* November 10, 1916.

6 "Who Re-elected the President," New York, *World,* November 11, 1916.

7 David J. Danelski and Joseph S. Tulchin, eds., *The Autobiographical Notes of Charles Evans Hughes* (Cambridge, Mass.: Harvard University Press, 1973), 184. Hughes kept blaming other people for his own failings, saying "Had I been warned," when his papers show warning signs galore. No one made him go to that pivotal anti-union luncheon in California.

8 James Laughlin Phillips to George Sutherland, November 11, 1916, George Sutherland Papers, Library of Congress.

9 William Howard Taft to Clarence Kelsey, November 18, 1916, William Howard Taft Papers, Library of Congress.

10 Theodore Roosevelt to William Willcox, November 29, 1916, Theodore Roosevelt Papers, Manuscript Division, Library of Congress.

11 Henry Cabot Lodge to Charles Evans Hughes, November 1916, Hughes Papers; Lodge to James Bryce, December 21, 1916, James Bryce Papers, Bodleian Library, Oxford, England.

12 Entry for December 2, 1916, in George F. Sparks, ed., *A Many-Colored Toga: The Diary of Henry Fountain Ashurst* (Tucson: University of Arizona Press, 1962), 50–51.

13 Charles W. Eliot to James Bryce, November 13, 1916, Bryce Papers.

14 John Milton Cooper, *Breaking the Heart of the World; Woodrow Wilson and the Fight for the League of Nations* (New York: Cambridge University Press, 2001), 390, note 25.

15 Randolph C. Downes, *The Rise of Warren Gamaliel Harding, 1865–1920* (Columbus: Ohio State University Press, 1970), 248, quotes Harding.

16 Theodore Roosevelt to Benjamin Ide Wheeler, November 29, 1916, Roosevelt Papers.

17 "New York Democrats to Roosevelt, November 10, 1916, copy in Hughes Papers.

18 Charles W. Eliot to James Bryce, November 13, 1916, Bryce Papers.

19 "Why Wilson Won," *Literary Digest* 53 (November 18, 1916).

20 Ibid.

21 "Women's Hand in the Election," *Literary Digest* (November 18, 1916): 1315–1316.

22 Edward C. McKay to F. M. Crossett, November 10, 1916, copy in Hughes Papers, is a good discussion of events in Ohio.

23 Walter Lippmann to Edward M. House, October 17, 1917, in Arthur S. Link et al., eds., *The Papers of Woodrow Wilson Volume 44: 1917* (Princeton, N.J.: Princeton University Press, 1983), 383.

24 Harold Ickes to James R. Garfield, February 18, 1918, Harold Ickes Papers, Library of Congress.

25 Will H. Hays, "The Republican Position," *Forum* 60 (August 1918): 136.

26 *New York Times*, November 11, 1916.

BIBLIOGRAPHICAL ESSAY

The manuscript sources for the election of 1916 are abundant. On the Democratic side, the key collections consists of the Woodrow Wilson Papers at the Manuscript Division of the Library of Congress (LC). The Wilson Papers have long been microfilmed and indexed, and are easy to use, though voluminous. Rivaling the Wilson Papers in importance are the Papers of Colonel Edward M. House, Sterling Library, Yale University. Other key Democratic collections are the papers of Newton D. Baker (LC), Josephus Daniels (LC), William G. McAdoo (LC), Thomas J. Walsh (LC), and Robert Woolley (LC).

On the Republican side, the papers of Charles Evans Hughes (LC) are valuable for the weaknesses of the Republican campaign. The Theodore Roosevelt Papers (LC) reflect Roosevelt's ambivalence about Hughes as a candidate and the former president's hatred of President Wilson. The William Howard Taft Papers (LC) have many interesting letters about the election and show Taft's dismay at the weaknesses of the Hughes campaign. The Henry Cabot Lodge Papers, Massachusetts Historical Society, reveal the animosity that Lodge felt toward Wilson. I was unable to locate any papers relating to the chair of the Hughes campaign, William R. Willcox, and his failings as a political organizer. The Lawrence Y. Sherman Papers at the Illinois State Library contain valuable documents on many aspects of the 1916 contest. Other collections on Republicans included the Charles W. Fairbanks Papers, Lilly Library, Indiana University; the Will H. Hays Papers, also at the Lilly Library; the John Wingate Weeks Papers at Dartmouth College; the Nicholas Murray Butler Papers, Columbia University; the George W. Perkins Papers, Columbia University; and the especially valuable James T. Williams, Jr. Papers, Duke University. The Francis B. Loomis Papers, Stanford University, available on microfilm, have several letters of interest about the campaign's fluctuating fortunes. The Erastus Brainerd Papers, University of Washington Library, have letters of Washington political reporters conveying information back to their employer with many useful insights.

Collections of published documents were very useful. Arthur S. Link and his colleagues at *The Papers of Woodrow Wilson, Volumes 31–38* (Princeton, N.J.: Princeton University Press, 1978–1982) made the task of the historian much easier with their wide-ranging compilation of relevant memoranda, documents, and letters from Wilson-related collections. Elting E. Morison et al., eds., *The Letters of Theodore Roosevelt, Volumes 7–8* (Cambridge, Mass.: Harvard University Press, 1953–1954), collected numerous letters about Roosevelt in the election of 1916, which make the positions of the former president very clear. There are no other published documentary collections of similar size and scope for participants in the 1916 election.

There is one published history of the 1916 election. S. D. Lovell, *The Presi-*

dential Election of 1916 (Carbondale: Southern Illinois University Press, 1980), is a slimmed-down version of a much longer dissertation. Lovell examines the contest as part of a triumph of progressive ideas over Republican opposition and somewhat underrates the extent of GOP hatred of the president and his administration. An unpublished study of considerable merit is Meyer Nathan, "The Presidential Election of 1916 in the Middle West," PhD dissertation, Princeton University, 1966.

Several articles have changed the manner in which historians view the 1916 contest. David Sarasohn, "The Election of 1916: Realigning the Rockies," *Western Historical Quarterly* 11 (1980): 285–305, saw long-term results from the success of Wilson in the West. William M. Leary, Jr., "Woodrow Wilson, Irish-Americans, and the Election of 1916," *Journal of American History* 56 (1967): 57–72, looks at Wilson's problems with a key voting bloc that did not turn out to be decisive when the votes were counted. Thomas J. Kerr IV, "German-Americans and Neutrality in the 1916 Election," *Mid-America* 43 (1961): 95–103, examines another key voting group. Robert P. Wilkins, "Referendum on War? The General Election of 1916 in North Dakota," *North Dakota History* 36 (1969): 52–76, looks at one key state in the West.

Biographies of the major figures in the 1916 election tend to focus on the victory of President Wilson. Arthur S. Link, *Wilson: Campaigns for Progressivism and Peace* (Princeton, N.J.: Princeton University Press, 1965), the final volume in Link's multivolume biography of Wilson, is excellent on the 1916 campaign from the president's point of view. John Milton Cooper, Jr., *Woodrow Wilson: A Biography* (New York: Alfred A. Knopf, 2009), has a perceptive discussion of the election in the context of Wilson's life. A. Scott Berg, *Wilson* (New York: G.P. Putnam's Sons, 2013), adds little to the accounts in Link and Cooper.

There is no modern biography of Charles Evans Hughes. The standard study of his life is Merlo Pusey, *Charles Evans Hughes*, 2 vols. (New York: Macmillan, 1951), and the coverage of 1916 reflects its subject's point of view. David J. Danelski and Joseph Tulchin, eds., *The Autobiographical Notes of Charles Evans Hughes* (Cambridge, Mass.: Harvard University Press, 1973), reveal a losing candidate who shifted blame for his defeat on to almost everyone but himself. James F. Simon, *FDR and Chief Justice Hughes: The President, the Supreme Court, and the Epic Battle over the New Deal* (New York: Simon & Schuster, 2012), has an interesting if not very penetrating chapter on Hughes as a presidential candidate. Robert F. Wesser, *Charles Evans Hughes: Politics and Reform in New York* (Ithaca, N.Y.: Cornell University Press, 1967), has some interesting insights into Hughes as governor.

The other major figure in the 1916 presidential election was Theodore Roosevelt. John Allen Gable, *The Bull Moose Years: Theodore Roosevelt and the Progressive Party* (Port Washington, N.Y.: Kennikat Press, 1978), does not have much on the 1916 campaign itself. Edmund Morris, *Colonel Roosevelt* (New York: Random House, 2010), considers 1916 from Roosevelt's point of view. J. Lee Thompson, *Never Call Retreat: Theodore Roosevelt and the Great War* (New York: Palgrave, 2013), is a pro-Roosevelt account that omits vital evidence. Lewis L. Gould, *From*

Chief Executive to Chief Justice: Taft from the White House to the Supreme Court (Lawrence: University Press of Kansas, 2014), considers how much the former president sought Wilson's defeat.

Very useful for the campaigning techniques of the Democrats in 1916 is Michael E. McGerr, *The Decline of Popular Politics: The American North, 1865–1928* (New York: Oxford University Press, 1986). Less helpful about the Democrats are: Douglas B. Craig, *Progressives at War: William G. McAdoo and Newton D. Baker* (Baltimore, Md.: Johns Hopkins University Press, 2013), and Lee A. Craig, *Josephus Daniels: His Life and Times* (Chapel Hill: University of North Carolina Press, 2013).

Because of the central role that the state of California played in the outcome of the election, commentators at the time and in the years that followed explored the relationship between Hiram Johnson and Charles Evans Hughes. Frederick M. Davenport, the New York Progressive who worked with Hughes, weighed in after the election in "The Case of Hiram Johnson—Not Guilty," *North American Review* (February 1917), and elaborated on the issue in "Did Hughes Snub Johnson?—An Inside Story: How and Why Charles Evans Hughes Lost California and the Presidency in 1916," *American Political Science Review* 43 (April 1949). An anti-Johnson essay is Alfred Holman, "The Case of Hiram Johnson—Guilty," *North American Review* (February 1917): 186–202. Spencer C. Olin, Jr., is the best modern student of the issue in "Hiram Johnson, the California Progressives, and the Hughes Campaign of 1916," *Pacific Historical Review* 31 (November 1962): 203–220, and *California's Prodigal Sons: Hiram Johnson and the Progressives, 1911–1917* (Berkeley: University of California Press, 1968).

Articles related to the 1916 contest include Elliott M. Rudwick, "East St. Louis and the 'Colonization Conspiracy' of 1916," *Journal of Negro Education* 33 (Winter 1964): 35–42; James Allen Beatson, "The Election the West Decided: 1916," *Arizona and the West* 3(Spring 1961): 39–58; and George C. Roberts, "Woodrow Wilson, John W. Kern, and the 1916 Indiana Election: Defeat of a Majority Leader," *Presidential Studies Quarterly* 10(Winter, 1980): 63–73.

There are many aspects of the election that could use scholarly scrutiny and the primary sources for such research are extensive. Among the most salient areas for further development are the internal workings of the Hughes campaign, the role of the tariff issue, the campaign in Ohio, and the success of the Democrats in the West.

INDEX